Designing and Implementing a Successful Undergraduate Research, Scholarship, and Creative Activity Program

Designing and Implementing a Successful Undergraduate Research, Scholarship, and Creative Activity Program is designed as a resource for faculty, administrators, and university leaders interested in developing new, or expanding existing, undergraduate research programs. The book provides a practical handbook addressing the many "how to" questions associated with running a successful undergraduate research enterprise – ranging from how to organize an undergraduate research office, to how to find funding, foster cross-campus relationships, and develop learning outcomes for students in order to maximize the benefits of the research experience. It also addresses best practices in mentoring, how faculty mentorship fits within the discussion of tenure and promotion, and the basics of assessment, for both funder reporting and program improvement.

Containing a series of vignettes offering specific advice from program directors, faculty mentors, and university administrators from a diverse array of universities and colleges, this book showcases their hands-on tips, advice, and lessons learned. Addressing key issues through real-world experience, the authors show how to build effective cross-disciplinary undergraduate research programs with positive impacts on students and faculty.

Dr. Holly E. Unruh is Executive Director of the Arts Research Institute at the University of California, Santa Cruz. She previously served as Associate Director of the Undergraduate Research Opportunities Center at California State University, Monterey Bay.

Dr. Heather Haeger is Research Director of the STEM Learning Center at the University of Arizona, and Assistant Professor of Educational Policy Studies and Practice. She served as the inaugural Assessment and Research Coordinator for the Council on Undergraduate Research from 2016 to 2020.

Dr. John E. Banks is Director of the Undergraduate Research Opportunities Center at California State University, Monterey Bay.

Dr. Winny Dong is Faculty Director of the Office of Undergraduate Research at Cal Poly Pomona and Professor of Chemical and Materials Engineering.

Routledge Undergraduate Research Series

Series Editors: Gregory Young, Montana State University and Jenny Olin Shanahan, Bridgewater State University

www.routledge.com/Routledge-Undergraduate-Research-Series/book-series/RURS

Designing and Implementing a Successful Undergraduate Research, Scholarship, and Creative Activity Program

Holly E. Unruh, Heather Haeger,
John E. Banks, and Winny Dong

NEW YORK AND LONDON

Designed cover image: © Getty Images

First published 2025
by Routledge
605 Third Avenue, New York, NY 10158

and by Routledge
4 Park Square, Milton Park, Abingdon, Oxon, OX14 4RN

Routledge is an imprint of the Taylor & Francis Group, an informa business

ISBN: 9780367724825 (hbk)
ISBN: 9780367724818 (pbk)
ISBN: 9781003154952 (ebk)

DOI: 10.4324/9781003154952

Typeset in Sabon
by Apex CoVantage, LLC

Contents

Acknowledgments

This volume brings together lessons we have collectively learned on the job, with what we see as current best practices in our field. We are deeply grateful to our colleagues, mentors, and communities of practice for the ways they have inspired us, modeled best practices, and been in conversation with us over the years. The book itself would not have been possible without the support, guidance, and generosity of several key people.

When Bill Head first hired Holly at California State University, Monterey Bay (CSUMB) nearly a decade ago, he told her she should "publish something about UROC." She didn't quite understand at the time what he meant. Our office, the Undergraduate Research Opportunities Center (UROC) at CSUMB, was the first centralized undergraduate research office organized within the 23-campus California State University (CSU) system when it was launched in 2009 and remains one of the more developed organizations in our system to this day. Needless to say, it only took a year or so at UROC for Bill's prompt to make sense, as we hosted visit after visit from colleagues across the country who wanted to learn about UROC and understand first-hand *how* we did what we did. So, thank you Bill for knowing years ago that this book needed to happen! We would also like to thank our series editors, Jenny Olin Shanahan and Gregory Young, for entertaining an email out of the blue with the suggestion that this kind of book – a bit different from the other, discipline-focused volumes they had edited – might make a good addition to the Routledge Undergraduate Research Series.

But most of all Holly, Heather, and John would like to thank our colleagues at UROC (some of whom have moved on to other institutions as academics are wont to do . . .), Bridgette Clarkston, Carla Fresquez, Natasha Oehlman, Bobby Quinoñez, and Megan Bassett, who were the "dream team" we had first had the privilege of working with at UROC. Their deep knowledge, professionalism, work ethic, and most of all sense of fun made UROC a terrific place to land. They were joined shortly by other colleagues who were equally instrumental in transforming our work, and continuing our focus on equity and student success: Eric Barajas, Meghan Stell, Suzanne Ocegura, Quentin Sedlacek, Corin Gray, Jessica Bautista, Rogers Walker, and Professor Corin Slown, who helped launch our work on CUREs. A special thanks goes out from Heather to Natasha Oehlman for helping her see herself as a writer and find her voice. She is also thankful for all of the undergraduate researchers, graduate students, and postdoctoral fellows that collaborated on her research. They have inspired her, kept her grounded, and brought so much joy into her life.

We would like to make special mention of two notable Provosts at CSUMB who were instrumental in facilitating the creation, growth, and persistence of UROC and helped elevate the profile of undergraduate research at CSUMB: Kathryn Cruz-Uribe, who was an early UROC champion, and Bonnie Irwin, who served as Provost at CSUMB from 2014 to 2019. We would also like to thank the Council on Undergraduate Research and especially Beth Ambos for believing in the value of research and assessment on URSCA and for investing in the Assessment and Research Coordination Fellowship, which was first held by Heather from 2016 to 2019. This fellowship gave her the time and space to focus on developing resources, many of which are now collected and referenced in this book.

Winny would like to thank Beth Ambos, Frank Ewers, and Jeff Marshall for planting the idea that there should be an Office of Undergraduate Research (OUR) at Cal Poly Pomona. When she founded that office in 2012 with a total budget of $72,000 (including salaries!), she had no idea how much it would grow and what an important role it would come to play in the lives of students, faculty, and the team that work for the OUR, including herself. She is also thankful for the team (both past and present) at the OUR at Cal Poly Pomona – none of what was accomplished would be possible without them.

Finally, we have some personal acknowledgments: [HU] I want to express my deep thanks and love to a few very special people outside of academia – Bobby Wrighton, Aiden Unruh, Alex Unruh, and Gary Unruh – you all keep me smiling, which in the end is the most important thing. [WD] Thank you to my amazing family who had nothing to do with this book. But you keep me humble by constantly pointing out my flaws and mistakes; you keep me happy by being unapologetically who you are; and you keep me sane by sharing your lives with me. I couldn't have contributed to this book without you because I would not be who I am without you. [JEB] Warmest thanks to the many mentors and colleagues who have inspired and influenced my journey in undergraduate research – including the late H.T. Banks. [HH] Thank you to Allison BrckaLorenz for finding ways to collaborate on URSCA research and for watching my son during many conference presentations. And, of course, thank you to my son, Allen. He was born the year I started my fellowship with Council on Undergraduate Research (CUR) and has attended more meetings and conferences than I can count. He has been cared for by a community of beautiful people who watch him while I conduct research, write about it, and present my research. My parents, Allen and Diane, have supported us through a pandemic and the struggles of being a working, single mother. And my dear friends, Morgan Galarza-Laska, Jamie Coracides, Claudia Sandoval, Nizhoni Chow-Garcia, Moria Ozias, and Z. Nicolazzo, who all support Allen and me and make this work possible.

Notes on contributors

Anne Boettcher, Assistant Dean of Research, Embry-Riddle Aeronautical University, Prescott Campus.

Kimberly Sierra-Cajas, Senior Director, STEM Equity Systems & Initiatives, University of Arizona.

John Celenza, Boston University Undergraduate Research Opportunities Program (UROP); Associate Professor of Biology; and Director, Program in Biochemistry & Molecular Biology.

Nura Dualeh (Director, Undergraduate Research and Graduate Preparation Programs, University of Arizona), **Andrew Huerta** (Director of the Ronald E. McNair Program, University of Arizona), **Victoria Juvera** (Office of Diversity and Inclusion, University of Arizona), **Holly Lopez** (Office of Diversity and Inclusion, University of Arizona), **Tianna Mac-Means** (Program Coordinator, UROC, University of Arizona), **Donna Treloar** (Director, Diversity Programs, University of Arizona), **Frans Tax** (Associate Dean, Student Affairs, Diversity & Inclusion, University of Arizona).

Cheryl Greengrove, Associate Vice-Chancellor for Research and Associate Professor of Geoscience, University of Washington, Tacoma.

Courtney Leligdon, Undergraduate Research Coordinator, University of Arizona.

Becky Green-Marroquin (Professor of Biology, Los Angeles Valley College) and **Pamela Byrd-Williams** (Professor of Biology, Los Angeles Valley College).

Ken O'Donnell, Vice Provost, California State University Dominguez Hills; and Editor-in-Chief, *Experiential Learning and Teaching in Higher Education.*

Jenny Olin Shanahan, Assistant Provost for High-Impact Practices, Bridgewater State University.

Marianne Smith, Director of the Institute for Completion, Citrus College, retired.

Candace Rypisi, Assistant Vice Provost and Director of Student–Faculty Programs at California Institute of Technology.

Yi-Chieh Wu (Associate Professor, Computer Science, Harvey Mudd College), **Katherine Van Heuvelen** (Associate Dean of Research and Experiential Learning, Harvey Mudd College) and **Nicole Wallens** (Director of Sponsored Research, Harvey Mudd College).

Melonie W. Sexton, Undergraduate Research Coordinator, DTC & WPC Social Science Coordinator, and Professor of Psychological Sciences, Valencia College, Orlando, Florida.

Beth Rushing, President, Appalachian College Association.

Colin Shaw, Director, Undergraduate Scholars Program; and Assistant Research Professor, Earth Sciences, Montana State University.

Series foreword

The Routledge Undergraduate Research Series was created to guide students and faculty through a wide variety of research and creative projects in diverse fields of study. Originally dedicated to undergraduate research in the fine and performing arts, the series has expanded to include programs in the humanities and education. Although academic disciplines outside the natural, physical, and social sciences have been underrepresented in many college and university research opportunities for undergraduate students, the global movement to expand access to undergraduate research is highly relevant to and powerfully transformational for students of all majors and programs. Each book in the series lays out stages of the research process in a particular discipline, with timely and applicable examples that illustrate common questions, considerations, and methods of scholars in the field. Chapter by chapter, the books show recursive and adaptable means of engaging in meaningful scholarship in the curriculum and co-curricular activities. The books are written for undergraduates as well as faculty, staff, and graduate-student mentors with varying levels of research and mentoring experience.

Gregory Young and Jenny Olin Shanahan
Series Editors

Foreword to the volume

Ken O'Donnell
Vice Provost, California State University, Dominguez Hills
Editor-in-Chief, *Experiential Learning and
Teaching in Higher Education*

College seems to be falling out of fashion just when we need it the most. Those of us who work in higher education probably had it coming: to us, the value of formal education after high school seems self-evident, so we're not always great at defending it. But to the rest of the world, we can come across as complacent, with irrelevant and overpriced thrown in. Student indebtedness is out of control, our calls for equity are drowned out by culture wars, and we've struggled to keep pace with the changing nature of our students, what they need, and how they learn.

At its best, college cultivates the curiosity, drive, and polymath fluency that make life full and interesting. Not incidentally, such habits also distinguish us from robots and AI, protecting our jobs in the face of technological change. And they equip us to talk to each other, collaborating across industries, disciplines, and cultures to address the existential threats that face us.

This makes it a particularly bad time for the world to lose its faith in us. These are challenging, harrowing times: social injustice, wealth inequality, climate change, and war are all interdisciplinary and wicked problems that can only be tackled collectively. The generations facing them next will be poorly served if they stop at high school, figuring they can pick up the rest of their education from their entry-level jobs, or on YouTube. It's a sign of our sector's stagnation, and cost, that those are increasingly attractive alternatives for students who used to come to us.

But solutions are at hand, and in fact already on our campuses. High-impact practices (HIPs) like learning communities, capstone courses, and community engagement get classes out of the rut of lecture, listen, memorize, repeat. They foreground the integrative creativity that characterizes the best of college and distinguishes it from other kinds of education. They illuminate the value of learning by asking students to apply it as they go along, to the real-world, unscripted problems they'll face after graduation. They are both our best offerings and our best selling points.

Savvy educators know this, across departments and divisions. With tools like ePortfolios and Comprehensive Learner Records, they are starting to pull experiential education out of the shadows, giving it the visibility and street cred that come with placement in a transcript or course catalog. It's turning up not just as extra credit for the students who know to look for it, but as a degree requirement for everyone. And as we make this progress, we destultify ourselves, recovering the purpose, spontaneity, and novelty that make learning valuable, and fun.

Foremost among those HIPs is student research, especially as offered to undergraduates. As humans, we owe our evolutionary success to our innate love of figuring things out together. Undergraduate research taps into those ancient urges, turbocharging student engagement. It makes learning thrilling, by giving each student the real opportunity to be the very first person who learns a particular thing, investigates it further, and then explains it to others. This is intellectual development in its natural state: purposeful, motivating, and social.

And among the HIPs, undergraduate research is especially valuable for casting postsecondary knowledge as a work in progress. It sidelines the rote learning and received wisdom available pretty much everywhere for free, shifting the emphasis to disciplinary ways of making sense of the world. At the edges of their understanding, we can see how various specialists think, where the unanswered questions lie, and what counts as evidence. The US baccalaureate is a degree of tentative specialization, blending broadly transferable general education with grounding in a major; students who conduct research understand in a very practical way the distinctive paradigms and perspectives that come with given discipline and get practice applying them.

But for all its value, undergraduate research is hard to offer. On the first try, most of us get it wrong, providing these experiences only rarely, or without adequate institutional support, or just to the overachievers with the nerve to ask. And so, for too much of their history, these practices have perpetuated privilege, at odds with our mission of egalitarian empowerment.

But then scaling it is just as problematic, requiring investments in infrastructure and faculty professional development that pay off only with sustained attention, over years.

Over the past 25 years or so, the California State University (CSU) collaborated with the Council on Undergraduate Research in a handful of multi-year, mostly grant-funded projects to try figuring this out together.

As a system of 23 regional comprehensive universities committed to access and equity, the CSU had much to gain. About one-third of its students are Asian or White; the rest are what other states call "under-represented minorities," in whom the CSU is happily awash. Most qualify for federal financial aid and will be the first in their families to earn a degree. For these students college isn't a given, even after they enroll; to serve them, we have to prove our value and relevance with every course, or they leave. Undergraduate research does this. And so bringing them into authentic research, scholarship, and creative activity isn't only in their interest; it's also in ours.

Across those years of partnership with the Council on Undergraduate Research (CUR), we learned a few things. For one, teaching this way is possible but not obvious, or easy; scaling research experiences is possible only with robust faculty professional development. For another, equitable research thrives in collaboration – with community partners, across disciplines, and above all with the student affairs offices who can raise its profile, by reaching students where they are.

To make these things happen, consistently and reliably, we saw that there is no substitute for a standing, permanently funded office for undergraduate research, scholarship, and creative activity. For an institution focused on access and affordability, this is bad news: betting on a permanent staff line is like planning to buy a house with your next winning lottery ticket. Yet on campus after campus, we saw that institutions that had scraped together one full-time-equivalent staff position, even at an entry-level classification, could make an outsized difference right away. Add a program head or reassigned faculty member and the benefits multiply again. And as you'll see here, you can then use the demonstrated interest from faculty and students to justify growing.

The CSU campuses represented here aren't a representative cross section. Monterey Bay and Pomona are institutions that do this especially well, making the wisdom here worth careful consideration, even if it's a little intimidating. But they got here piece by piece, over many years and through successive administrative regimes. What's striking about this book is that it shows us exactly how they did it. The chapters on the first year, and finding sustainable funding, are revelations. Vignettes along the way show how very different institutions, ranging from open-access community colleges to hyper-selective elites, have pulled this off, making small but strategic investments in communication, outreach, and evidence-gathering to support growth.

The bottom line: creating such an office requires stamina on the part of its champions and courage from leadership – especially in a time of shrinking budgets and enrollment. But what you'll see here is that hard isn't the same as impossible, and it's surprisingly effective to start small.

Along the way, the institutions that offer this kind of education will be rediscovering with their students one of the most important things about college in the first place: its unmatched knack for orchestrating learning that's creative, social, vitally important, and fun, all at the same time, at a time when we need it most.

There's a lot at stake, and not just for higher education. It's time to turn the page, take a breath, and jump.

1 The importance of undergraduate research, scholarship, and creative activity

I am a student who participated in the life-changing research program (CCARE) [the Community College Apprentice Research Experience program] . . . I am writing to express my sincere gratitude for accepting me to the program and for all the generous help. I was a returning student in community college at the time because I was too tired of working minimum wage jobs here and there. This program allowed me to dream and boosted my confidence in merely three months. I just graduated with departmental honors at UCLA and am starting my Chemical Engineering graduate program this fall!

Quote from alum of the California State University,
Monterey Bay, Undergraduate Research Opportunities
Center program

There is a wealth of literature describing the impact of undergraduate research, scholarship, and creative activity (URSCA) on student success and persistence. In addition to the gains students experience in their critical thinking skills, disciplinary identity, and self-confidence as academics, the process of digging into research is often one of the most joyous and fulfilling things students experience during their undergraduate years. Thinking of URSCA as a pedagogical approach to teaching and learning, the Council on Undergraduate Research (CUR) defines undergraduate research as: *A mentored investigation or creative inquiry conducted by undergraduates that seeks to make a scholarly or artistic contribution to knowledge.* URSCA is well established as a high-impact practice (HIP) because of its rigorous and high expectations, the necessity of collaboration with faculty mentors, emphasis on problem-solving in a real-world context, and the importance it places on the public dissemination of knowledge.[1] Research has shown that undergraduate research and creative scholarship increases student engagement, creates opportunities for applied and hands-on learning, and fosters academic success including increased grade point average (GPA), retention, and persistence.[2]

DOI: 10.4324/9781003154952-1

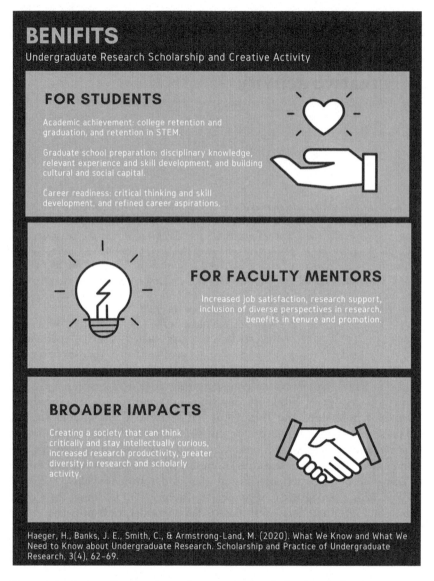

Haeger, H., Banks, J. E., Smith, C., & Armstrong-Land, M. (2020). What We Know and What We Need to Know about Undergraduate Research. Scholarship and Practice of Undergraduate Research, 3(4), 62–69.

Figure 1.1 The benefits of undergraduate research, scholarship, and creative activity
(URSCA). Based on a review of literature on URSCA.[3]

Disrupting patterns of inequality

Colleges and universities are deeply concerned about the retention and
graduation rates of their students. We have found that supporting participation in undergraduate research is one of the most powerful tools an

institution has to move the needle on these numbers. Many students who pursue a college degree never finish that degree. An incoming student at a public US four-year college has only a 36% chance of graduating in four years and a 59% chance of graduating in six years.[4] The odds of completing a college degree are even lower for students who have been traditionally marginalized and underserved in higher education.[5] For example, low and middle-socioeconomic status (SES) students graduate at much lower rates than their high-SES peers; only 40–50% of those students will attain a bachelor's degree within ten years compared to 74% of high-SES students.[6]

URSCA has been shown to be particularly beneficial to low- to middle-SES students, as well as first-generation college students, and students of color, so much so that participation has been shown to have a compensatory effect; in other words, these students can see an even greater benefit from engagement in undergraduate research in terms of grades and retention.[7] This effect can be seen in the dramatic impact undergraduate research experiences have on college completion rates.

We conducted an analysis of the experiences of 43,559 first-year college students at or below the poverty level which demonstrates the dramatic potential for change that undergraduate research can have.[8] When low-income students participate in URSCA, the number of students who stop out without a degree is extremely low. The vast majority (95%) of these students go on to graduate from college in six years or less. This is in stark contrast to the numbers for students who do *not* participate in URSCA. For every 100 of those students who enter college, 43 do not make it to graduation and 41 will never go on to attain a college degree (see Figures 1.2 and 1.3).

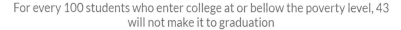

For every 100 students who enter college at or bellow the poverty level, 43 will not make it to graduation

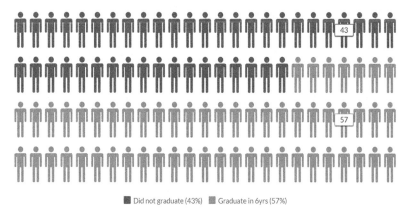

■ Did not graduate (43%)   ■ Graduate in 6yrs (57%)

Figure 1.2 Six-year graduation rates for college students at or below the poverty level.

For every 100 undergraduate researchers who enter college at or bellow the poverty level, 95 will graduate in 6 years or less

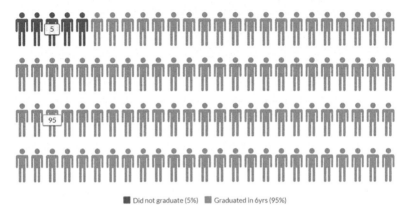

■ Did not graduate (5%)   ■ Graduated in 6yrs (95%)

Figure 1.3 Six-year graduation rates for undergraduate researchers at or below the poverty level.

Participation in URSCA can also disrupt patterns of inequality by promoting more equitable student access to specific forms of economic, social, and cultural capital.[9] For example, low-SES students often do not have the time or financial resources to be able to engage in any additional unpaid academic work – for example, internships, research, and other field-specific opportunities for direct hands-on learning. When these students have access to paid research opportunities, we have found that they can often afford to forego a job that has little to do with their academic work (in other words, stop working at Starbucks), in favor of pursuing a research opportunity that will take them much further in the academic realm, while still allowing them to add to or maintain their personal finances.

Studies have also shown that building social relationships, or what we are calling social capital, helps students to develop strong identities as researchers and alleviates their uncertainty about their sense of belonging within the institution or their discipline, leading them to respond to challenges and adversity in adaptive ways.[10] URSCA can support the development of this social capital in several ways. For example, students who participate in mentored undergraduate research often have transformative experiences collaborating with university faculty, and even more positive experiences working with both faculty and graduate students or post-doctoral researchers.[11] Furthermore, these social relationships can cultivate students' underlying motivations for learning different disciplinary knowledge or skills. For students who work in courses, labs, or research teams with fellow undergraduates, group activities with peers also contribute to interpersonal relationships that support their sense of self-efficacy, short-term learning, and long-term academic success.[12]

Research experiences can also directly or indirectly help students develop numerous forms of cultural capital valued by the university. These include resiliency and problem-solving strategies, critical skills like communication and teamwork, a greater sense of identification with their field, and a feeling of preparedness for graduate education.[13] Ultimately, these experiences show tremendous benefit to historically excluded students and help reduce achievement gaps between these students and their traditionally privileged peers.[14]

Identifying barriers to participation

Despite the great benefits of URSCA for all students, research shows that students who have been traditionally excluded from higher education based on their race, ethnicity, or socioeconomic status are far less likely to participate in the practice than their peers, even when attending a Hispanic-Serving Institution (HSI) or Minority-Serving Institution (MSI).[15] Additionally, historically excluded students may find a research culture that presents an unsupportive or even hostile environment.[16] In order to interrupt patterns of exclusion and increase equitable engagement in undergraduate research, it is important that colleges and universities work to both increase access to student opportunities and create inclusive research environments for diverse students and their faculty mentors.

In a survey of students at California State University, Monterey Bay, 94% of students stated that they believed that undergraduate research would help them achieve their career goals. Despite the fact that the vast majority of students saw the value of these experiences, by the time of graduation, only around 25% had participated in a mentored research experience.[17] These numbers are representative of the case across the country (Figure 1.4). One of the reasons for this dichotomy is a lack of access to research experiences. This can be caused by the limited number of mentored research experiences, difficulty in finding mentored research experiences, and other barriers like financial or time constraints, which make participation unfeasible.[18] Many students also report that they don't see themselves as researchers, and that attaining that goal seems out of reach for "someone like me."

For example, faculty are more likely to initiate mentoring relationships with students that they relate to or feel commonality with. The lack of diversity in the professoriate perpetuates the engagement of traditionally privileged students in URSCA. Additionally, students who are the first in

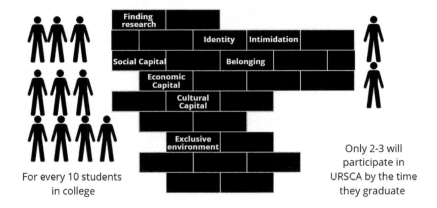

For every 10 students in college

Only 2-3 will participate in URSCA by the time they graduate

Figure 1.4 Barriers that block students from participating in undergraduate research, scholarship, and creative activity.

their family to go to college and whose high schools do not have a strong college-going culture might not understand the hidden curriculum (e.g., knowing what URSCA is and how to find opportunities) or have access to the cultural and social capital (e.g., exposure to potential research-related careers or social connections to people in those careers). It is crucial to understand your student population. Who is currently included in research, scholarship, and creativity activity at your institution, at both the faculty and undergraduate levels? Once you understand who is included and who might be excluded, you can create programs and policies to encourage more equitable participation. Removing the need to seek out research opportunities on an individual level by embedding research in the curriculum and centralizing support for research can help pave the way for more diverse populations of students to engage in URSCA.

Maximizing access: Course-based Undergraduate Research Experiences (CUREs)

Colleges and universities can combat many of the barriers addressed here by embedding research opportunities in the curriculum through Course-based Undergraduate Research Experiences (CUREs). Embedding research in the curriculum removes barriers related to cultural capital (students do not need to know how to find research opportunities), social capital (they do not need to have previous relationships with faculty mentors), and economic capital (they do not need to divert time away from work or other commitments to participate in URSCA since it is part of their coursework).

Chapter 12 will provide more details on how to support CURE development and scaffold CUREs across the curriculum.

There is a robust movement to incorporate CUREs into the community college curriculum. As faculty at two-year colleges are not required to do research to get tenure, the mechanisms for including students in, and introducing students to, research are often quite different from what we might expect to see at four-year institutions. The Community College Undergraduate Research Initiative (CCURI) is currently undertaking a study of its partners to try to understand the conditions that lead to successful research programs at community colleges.[19] In 2019, CCURI partnered with the American Association of Community Colleges (AACU) on a Community Colleges Undergraduate Research Experiences Summit. While focused largely on undergraduate research experiences in STEM, discussants at the conference identified several key factors that they believe contribute to successful undergraduate research endeavors at the community college level; the most important being "their alignment with the college's strategic plan and the support they receive from college administrators . . . . "[20] They also created a comprehensive list of recommendations to help scale and sustain and ensure equitable access to undergraduate research experiences.

Additionally, in our home state of California, the honors programs at various California Community Colleges (CCCs) are tied to the University of California honors program in order to promote student research, and each year there is a student research conference at the University of California, Irvine.[21] The community college baccalaureate programs (there are currently 15 across the state) also promote student research as a key component of these new four-year degrees.[22]

A centralized office

In addition to embedding undergraduate research, scholarship, and creative activity in the curriculum, creating a centralized URSCA office can reduce barriers in a number of ways including creating a more user-friendly mechanism for students to approach research engagement. In surveys and focus groups with students on our home campus at California State University, Monterey Bay, we found that while many students expressed an interest in research, many of them did not pursue an opportunity because they were intimidated both by the idea of research and by the daunting task of approaching faculty and/or identifying an independent project of their own to work on.[23] A centralized office can also coordinate outreach efforts so that more students are aware of research opportunities and broaden their view of what they might engage with. Perhaps the most important function a centralized office can play is in providing support to students to help them build the social and cultural capital needed to engage in URSCA (Figure 1.5). This can be done through research or social events that connect students to other students, to graduate students, and to faculty conducting research – or through specific trainings and resources aimed at helping students find research opportunities.

Across the country, URSCA programs are developing support programs intended to recruit students into URSCA, and let them get a glimpse of what the practice might look like in their discipline, as a way of overcoming that intimidation factor (Figure 1.6). At CSUMB and other institutions, URSCA offices have created *Research Rookies* programs that introduce students to what research and scholarship look like in their discipline

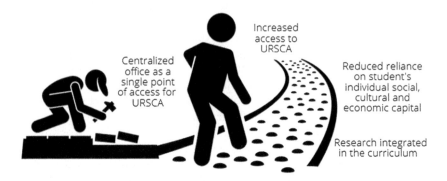

Figure 1.5 Creating pathways to engagement through CUREs and centralized URSCA offices.

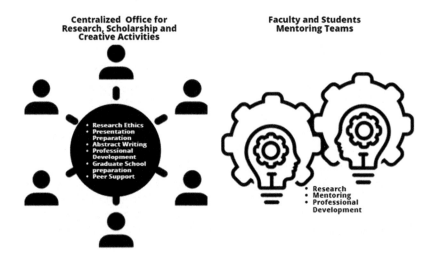

Figure 1.6 Points of alignment for a centralized office.

without the pressure of finding a mentored research experience on their own. Our own *Research Rookies* program provides online modules (e.g., Responsible Conduct of Research training), in-person social and research events (e.g., Coffee with a Research and research showcases and symposia), and activities for students to complete (e.g., interview two faculty about how they found their research interest, participate in a citizen science project). These serve to build cultural and social capital around research and provide a structure for learning about opportunities on campus.

Beyond the benefits to students, creating a centralized office for undergraduate research, scholarship, and creative activity can add value to the campus, focusing on providing assistance to offset the faculty workload, ensuring even distribution of information and resources, and reducing the duplication of efforts. For example, providing ethics training or support for research presentation design can reduce faculty workload and prevent each lab, department, or research group on campus from having to create their own resources and training for students. Centralizing the professional development and student support in one place on campus allows faculty to focus their time and attention on the critical task of providing socioemotional and research mentoring for students.

Additionally, a centralized resource center can connect students to faculty and campus to the national conversation. This can be done through fostering research events regionally and connecting students and faculty to national conference and publication opportunities.

Disciplinary inclusion: research, mentorship, and support in the arts, humanities, and social sciences

Though many undergraduate research programs focus on students in STEM disciplines, students can engage in authentic research, scholarship, and knowledge production in every discipline. We encourage you to familiarize yourself with the research process in various fields as you think about developing your programs. The Routledge Undergraduate Research Series offers a number of volumes designed to guide students and faculty, particularly in the arts and humanities, working on a wide variety of research and creative projects. After a brief overview, chapters on the research process common to all disciplines follow, and then several chapters that pertain specifically to the discipline.[24]

We encourage you to add these to your library. A common pitfall in creating a centralized office to support URSCA is creating infrastructure, programs, and policies based on a narrow conceptualization of what undergraduate research looks like based on STEM research experiences. An example of this might be the creation of a centralized summer program for students engaging in URSCA that is built around a lab-based research experience. Often these include ten weeks of required, weekly workshops and a cumulative presentation of work at a campus symposium at the end. But how does such a program work for students in the humanities who may need to travel to access archives over the summer? Can they participate in this program if they have to miss half the sessions? What about a student who is working with a youth community arts program? It is important to recognize and accommodate the possibility that the student, their mentor, and community partners may create a public performance as their culminating experience, but not have a poster to present at the end of the summer symposium.

Research, scholarship, and creative activity in the arts, humanities, and social sciences may also run on a different time scale than STEM fields. While a student in STEM may be able to join a lab and conduct an experiment using data already being collected so that they have a completed project to present at the end of one summer, in the social sciences, students and faculty may spend the majority of the summer conceptualizing a study, designing instruments and protocols, and submitting an Institutional Review Board (IRB) protocol. Students in the arts and humanities may spend the majority of a summer completing a literature review and building the community connections necessary to create a collaborative project or gain access to private or community archives. When you create a centralized program like these summer workshop series and seminars, consider how students in all disciplines might engage with the program and need support. Are there ways to be flexible to allow for different types of experiences? How can you solicit feedback from students and faculty to create programs and policies that work across disciplines?

The rich diversity of what URSCA can look like across disciplines can be a challenge when colleges and universities try to define what is and isn't research or scholarly activities. Initial definitions tend to revolve around the scientific process and aren't inclusive of what URSCA might look like in the arts, humanities, and social sciences. As you centralize support for URSCA, don't get stuck debating what "counts" as research or not. Instead of getting stuck in defining URSCA in each discipline, adopt a broad and inclusive definition (see CUR's definition earlier in this chapter) and allow faculty and students in each discipline to engage in authentic, disciplinary work together.[25] Resources for campus leadership and faculty to learn more about how URSCA experiences in the arts, humanities, and social sciences include:

- The Routledge Undergraduate Research Series (www.routledge.com/ Routledge-Undergraduate-Research-Series/book-series/RURS) includes books on undergraduate research across discipline and in the arts, humanities, and social sciences (e.g., undergraduate research in music, dance, architecture, education, humanities, theater, history, language, and religious studies). Accessing these publications as you create an URSCA center can help create programs and policies that work across disciplines. Additionally, students and faculty in these disciplines may use them as they think about creating more URSCA opportunities for students in the arts, humanities, and social sciences.

- CUR provides a number of resources for participating institutions or individual members about URSCA in the arts, humanities, and social sciences. They also have a number of publications about URSCA across disciplines and within specific disciplines (https://myaccount.cur.org/bookstore). For example, *Creative Inquiry in the Arts & Humanities: Models of Undergraduate Research* (2011) provides useful information for faculty and for those supporting URSCA.
- Many URSCA programs have curated examples of what URSCA looks like in different disciplines. The *Research in . . .* series from the Office of Undergraduate Research at Northwestern (https://undergradresearch.northwestern.edu/advising/our-videos/) has interviews with faculty and students about what research looks like in 15 different disciplines.

In centralizing support for URSCA across disciplines, it is also helpful to focus on the goals that your students and institution have for research, scholarship, and creative experiences. How should students engage in their discipline, how will they connect to faculty or their peers, and what will they gain from these experiences? Defining common goals, values, and outcomes for URSCA experiences can be more productive than belaboring specific criteria to define what is or isn't an URSCA experience. In Chapter 11, we provide more insight into assessing undergraduate research, and creating this type of consensus around goals can also aid in deciding what to measure and how to do so, in order to assess your programs.

VIGNETTE 1.1   Centralizing support for URSCA at the University of Arizona, a large, public, Hispanic-Serving Institution

Nura Dualeh, Andrew Huerta, Victoria Juvera, Holly Lopez, Tianna MacMeans, Donna Treloar, Frans Tax, University of Arizona

Recruitment

The goal of the University of Arizona (UArizona) Undergraduate Research Opportunities Consortium (UROC) is to increase graduate school access for students from groups underrepresented in graduate education. One mechanism that UROC uses to inform prospective students about its programs is its website (https://grad.arizona.edu/ diversityprograms/uroc), which emphasizes access to students from underrepresented groups and extolls the benefits of participating in UROC activities, including:

- research experience under the guidance of a faculty mentor.
- professional development and graduate admission workshops.
- social networking and community building with like-minded peers.
- poster session, oral presentation, and abstract writing.
- a free comprehensive GRE test preparation workshop.
- a $5,000* summer stipend.

To further publicize UROC programs, the Graduate College Diversity Programs Staff uses six approaches: (1) recruiting out-of-state students through attendance at meetings such as Society for the Advancement of Chicanos and Native Americans in Science (SACNAS), American Indians in Science & Engineering Society (AISES), Annual Biomedical Research Conference for Minority Students (ABRCMS), and the California Diversity Forums; (2) presentations to UArizona programs and classes and cultural centers, including a class for prospective Pima College transfer students, Arizona Science Engineering and Math Scholars, and to other research programs such as Undergraduate Readying for Burgeoning Research for American Indian Neuroscientists (URBRAIN), and Native American Cancer Prevention Program (NACP) (3) we also offer Gear Up for Graduate School Workshops, which are virtual open houses with staff and alumni present to answer questions (https://grad.arizona.edu/diversityprograms/preparation/ gear-graduate-school-workshops-0); (4) advertising for paid summer internships on the Handshake platform; (5) using Slate.org electronic campaigns to targeted groups of students; (6) we also take advantage of our networks of former undergraduates and graduate students to get the word out.

Application

The Graduate College Diversity Programs Staff emphasizes holistic admissions practices in the design of the UROC application. These holistic admissions practices specifically exclude components that are typically part of many research program applications. Because UROC's goal is to provide underserved students with their first paid research experience, previous research experience, transcripts, and letters of reference are not required. In addition, since many community college transfer students apply within their first semester after transferring, no official UArizona course grades are required. Instead, in the application, students are asked to respond to a series of prompts with choices of fill-in-the-blank answers and pull-down options for demographic and other descriptive information that covers student financial need, whether the student is a first-generation college student or a member of an ethnic group under-represented in their discipline. Next, students are asked to respond to a series of short answer prompts that query their previous academic, research, work, and/or volunteer experiences. They also have an optional question they can address: *Expand on how the group to which you belong is considered underrepresented in graduate education.* Students can then include other identities or intersectionalities that were not specifically addressed such as a disability, being a member of the LGBTQIA community, or any other under-representation they list.

Because writing personal statements does not come easily to many students, particularly those from underrepresented groups, the prompts for the personal statement are designed to bring out the four most important elements: background information, the specific research interests of the student, the reasons for wanting to attend graduate school (and post-graduate plans), and, finally, querying what the student plans to gain from UROC. Finally, the UROC application, including all prompts and questions, is always fully visible to students. This allows students to plan to complete the application without hidden or surprise questions.

The last component of the holistic review is an interview with one or two of the UROC staff. We ask the students to bring unofficial transcripts (free to the student). During the interview, we ask the student to share the "story of the transcript." This gives them a chance to discuss the strategies they used during their strong semesters, as well as the challenges they faced as indicated by any weak grades. The interview is enriched by the transcript review. So much so that if a student is not accepted, they still have benefited from discussing their transcript with experienced graduate school recruiters. The conversation oftentimes centers on their graduate school aspirations. Applicants begin to realize their "strengths" as articulated by the UROC team. In addition, when it comes to any areas that need improvement, they discover additional strategies they can use to strengthen their UROC application and by extension, their upcoming graduate school applications.

Notes

1 Kuh, G.D. *High-Impact Educational Practices: What They Are, Who Has Access to Them, and Why They Matter*. Association of American Colleges and Universities, 2008.

2 Kinzie, J., et al. "Promoting Persistence and Success of Underrepresented Students: Lessons for Teaching and Learning." *New Directions for Teaching and Learning*, vol. 2008 no. 115, 2008, 21–38, https://doi.org/10.1002/tl.323
   Laursen, S. *Undergraduate Research in the Sciences Engaging Students in Real Science*. John Wiley & Sons, Inc., 2010, www.CSUMB.eblib.com/patron/FullRecord.aspx?p=547064
   Haeger, H., and C. Fresquez. "Mentoring for Inclusion: The Impact of Mentoring on Undergraduate Researchers in the Sciences." *CBE-Life Sciences Education*, vol. 15 no. 3, 2016, ar36, https://doi.org/10.1187/cbe.16-01-0016
   Russell, C.B., and G.C. Weaver. "A Comparative Study of Traditional, Inquiry-Based, and Research-Based Laboratory Curricula: Impacts on Understanding of the Nature of Science." *Chemistry Education Research and Practice*, vol. 12 no. 1, 2011, 57–67, https://doi.org/10.1039/C1RP90008K

3 Haeger, H., et al. "What We Know and What We Need to Know About Undergraduate Research." *Scholarship and Practice of Undergraduate Research*, vol. 3 no. 4, 2020, 62–69.

4 National Academies of Sciences Engineering, and Medicine. (2017). *Undergraduate Research Experiences for STEM Students: Successes, Challenges, and Opportunities*. https://doi.org/10.17226/24622

5 Manzoni, A., and J. Streib. "The Equalizing Power of a College Degree for First-Generation College Students: Disparities Across Institutions, Majors, and Achievement Levels." *Research in Higher Education*, vol. 60 no. 5, 2019, 577–605, https://doi.org/10.1007/s11162-018-9523-1
   Stephens, N M., et al. "Closing the Social-Class Achievement Gap: A Difference-Education Intervention Improves First-Generation Students' Academic Performance and All Students' College Transition." *Psychological Science*, vol. 25 no. 4, 2014, 943–953, https://doi.org/10.1177/0956797613518349
   Wilbur, T.G., and V.J. Roscigno. "First-Generation Disadvantage and College Enrollment/Completion." *Socius*, vol. 2, 2016, https://doi.org/10.1177/2378023116664351

6 Kena, G., et al. "The Condition of Education 2015." *National Center for Education Statistics*, vol. 320, 2015.
   SES – measured as parental education and income – note 40% for low income and 50% for middle income.

7 Jones, M.T., et al. "Importance of Undergraduate Research for Minority Persistence and Achievement in Biology." *Journal of Higher Education*, vol. 81 no. 1, 2010, 82–115.

8 Haeger, H. "Measuring the Impact of Undergraduate Research: A Quasi-Experimental Study." Paper Presented at the Association for the Study of Higher Education, 2019.

9 Aikens, M.L. *A Social Capital Perspective on the Mentoring of Undergraduate Life Science Researchers: An Empirical Study of Undergraduate-Postgraduate-Faculty Triads*, 2016, https://doi.org/10.1187/cbe.15-10-0208
   Thompson, J.J., and D. Jensen-Ryan. "Becoming a 'Science Person': Faculty Recognition and the Development of Cultural Capital in the Context of Undergraduate Biology Research." *CBE—Life Sciences Education*, vol. 17 no. 4, 2018, ar62, https://doi.org/10.1187/cbe.17-11-0229

10 Robnett, R.D., et al. "Longitudinal Associations Among Undergraduates' Research Experience, Self-Efficacy, and Identity." *Journal of Research in Science Teaching*, vol. 52 no. 6, 2015, 847–867, https://doi.org/10.1002/tea.21221

11 Olivares-Donoso, R., and C. González. "Undergraduate Research or Research-Based Courses: Which Is Most Beneficial for Science Students?" *Research in Science Education*, vol. 49 no. 1, 2019, 91–107, https://doi.org/10.1007/s11165-017-9616-4
   Aikens, M.L., et al. *A Social Capital Perspective on the Mentoring of Undergraduate Life Science Researchers: An Empirical Study of Undergraduate-Postgraduate-Faculty Triads*, 2016, https://doi.org/10.1187/cbe.15-10-0208

12 Cohen, E., et al. "Complex Instruction: Equity in Cooperative Learning Classrooms." *Theory Into Practice-Theory Pract*, vol. 38, 1999, 80–86, https://doi.org/10.1080/00405849909543836.

13 Carter, D.F., et al. "Undergraduate Research Experiences in Promoting Engineering Students' Communication, Teamwork, and Leadership Skills." *Research in Higher Education*, vol. 57 no. 3, 2016, 363–393.
   Hurtado, S., et al. "Training Future Scientists: Predicting First-Year Minority Student Participation in Health Science Research." *Research in Higher Education*, vol. 49 no. 2, 2008, 126–152.

14 Kinzie, J., et al. "Promoting Persistence and Success of Underrepresented Students: Lessons for Teaching and Learning." *New Directions for Teaching and Learning*, vol. 2008 no. 115, 2008, 21–38, https://doi.org/10.1002/tl.323

15 National Academy of Sciences, et al. *Expanding Underrepresented Minority Participation: America's Science and Technology Talent at the Crossroads*. The National Academies Press, 2011, https://doi.org/10.17226/12984
   Haeger, H., et al. "Participation in Undergraduate Research at Minority Serving Institutions." *Perspectives on Undergraduate Research and Mentoring*, vol. 4 no. 1, 2015, http://blogs.elon.edu/purm/files/2015/11/Haeger-et-al-PURM-4.1-1.pdf

16 Clancy, K.B.H., et al. "Survey of Academic Field Experiences (SAFE): Trainees Report Harassment and Assault." *PLoS One*, vol. 9 no. 7, 2014, e102172, https://doi.org/10.1371/journal.pone.0102172

17 Haeger, H., et al. "Participation in Undergraduate Research at Minority Serving Institutions." *Perspectives on Undergraduate Research and Mentoring*, vol. 4 no. 1, 2015.

18 Figure 3 based on research from: Haeger, H., et al. "Creating More Inclusive Research Environments for Undergraduates." *Journal of the Scholarship of Teaching and Learning*, vol. 21 no. 1, 2021, Article 1, https://doi.org/10.14434/josotl.v21i1.30101

19 www.ccuri.us/

20 www.aacc.nche.edu/wp-content/uploads/2020/04/AACC_URE_Summit_Executive_Summary_Final2.pdf

21 See www.honorstransfercouncil.org/the-conference-1

22 On September 28, 2014, California Governor Jerry Brown signed Senate Bill 850 (Block, 2014) authorizing the California Community Colleges Board of Governors to establish the statewide baccalaureate degree pilot program at 15 California community colleges. In November 2014, the California Community Colleges Chancellor's Office Academic Affairs division sought applications from colleges that were interested in participating in the bachelor's degree pilot program. In May 2015, the Board of Governors approved 15 colleges to

participate in the pilot program. The first Bachelor's Degree Program graduates received their degrees in spring 2018.
www.cccco.edu/About-Us/Chancellors-Office/Divisions/Educational-Services-and-Support/What-we-do/Curriculum-and-Instruction-Unit/Curriculum/Baccalaureate-Degree-Pilot-Program

23 Haeger, H., et al. "What We Know and What We Need to Know About Undergraduate Research." *Scholarship and Practice of Undergraduate Research*, vol. 3 no. 4, 2020, 62–69.

24 See www.routledge.com/Routledge-Undergraduate-Research-Series/book-series/RURS?gclid=CjwKCAiAu9yqBhBmEiwAHTx5p76cnVxSvSOISrY8zwnBt8UsZC02nB-8K0dboM1qnT_P5qb5iIAD-BoCm-kQAvD_BwE

25 Alongside our recommendation that you work with the most expansive definition of URSCA as possible, we will note that our own system (the California State University) has developed some language to help students and their mentors understand the stages through which a student researcher might grow – from novice to advanced. We include this taxonomy at the end of this chapter for reference.

References

Aikens, M.L., et al. "A Social Capital Perspective on the Mentoring of Undergraduate Life Science Researchers: An Empirical Study of Undergraduate-Postgraduate-Faculty Triads." 2016, https://doi.org/10.1187/cbe.15-10-0208

California State University Undergraduate Research, Scholarship, and Creative Activities Taxonomy (Revised Draft, October 2016).

Carter, D.F., et al. "Undergraduate Research Experiences in Promoting Engineering Students' Communication, Teamwork, and Leadership Skills." *Research in Higher Education*, vol. 57 no. 3, 2016, 363–393.

CCURI | Undergraduate Research | United States. "CCURI." n.d., www.ccuri.us/. Accessed 26 January 2024.

Clancy, K.B.H., et al. "Survey of Academic Field Experiences (SAFE): Trainees Report Harassment and Assault." *PLoS One*, vol. 9 no. 7, 2014, e102172, https://doi.org/10.1371/journal.pone.0102172

Cohen, E., et al. "Complex Instruction: Equity in Cooperative Learning Classrooms." *Theory Into Practice—Theory Pract*, vol. 38, 1999, 80–86, https://doi.org/10.1080/00405849909543836

Haeger, H. "Measuring the Impact of Undergraduate Research: A Quasi-Experimental Study." Paper presented at the Association for the Study of Higher Education, 2019.

Haeger, H., et al. "Participation in Undergraduate Research at Minority Serving Institutions." *Perspectives on Undergraduate Research and Mentoring*, vol. 4 no. 1, 2015, http://blogs.elon.edu/purm/files/2015/11/Haeger-et-al-PURM-4.1-1.pdf

Haeger, H., et al. "What We Know and What We Need to Know About Undergraduate Research." *Scholarship and Practice of Undergraduate Research*, vol. 3 no. 4, 2020, 62–69.

Haeger, H., et al. "Creating More Inclusive Research Environments for Undergraduates." *Journal of the Scholarship of Teaching and Learning*, vol. 21 no. 1, 2021, Article 1, https://doi.org/10.14434/josotl.v21i1.30101

Haeger, H., and C. Fresquez. "Mentoring for Inclusion: The Impact of Mentoring on Undergraduate Researchers in the Sciences." *CBE-Life Sciences Education*, vol. 15 no. 3, 2016, ar36, https://doi.org/10.1187/cbe.16-01-0016

Honors Transfer Council of California | The Conference. "HTCC." n.d., www.honorstransfercouncil.org/the-conference-1. Accessed 26 January 2024.

Hurtado, S., et al. "Training Future Scientists: Predicting First-Year Minority Student Participation in Health Science Research." *Research in Higher Education*, vol. 49 no. 2, 2008, 126–152.

Jones, M.T., et al. "Importance of Undergraduate Research for Minority Persistence and Achievement in Biology." *Journal of Higher Education*, vol. 81 no. 1, 2010, 82–115.

Kena, G., et al. "The Condition of Education 2015." *National Center for Education Statistics*, vol. 320, 2015.

Kinzie, J., et al. "Promoting Persistence and Success of Underrepresented Students: Lessons for Teaching and Learning." *New Directions for Teaching and Learning*, vol. 2008 no. 115, 2008, 21–38, https://doi.org/10.1002/tl.323

Kuh, G.D. *High—Impact Educational Practices: What They Are, Who Has Access to Them, and Why They Matter.* Association of American Colleges and Universities, 2008.

Laursen, S. *Undergraduate Research in the Sciences Engaging Students in Real Science.* John Wiley & Sons, Inc., 2010, www.CSUMB.eblib.com/patron/FullRecord.aspx?p=547064

Manzoni, A., and J. Streib. "The Equalizing Power of a College Degree for First-Generation College Students: Disparities Across Institutions, Majors, and Achievement Levels." *Research in Higher Education*, vol. 60 no. 5, 2019, 577–605, https://doi.org/10.1007/s11162-018-9523-1

National Academy of Sciences, et al. *Expanding Underrepresented Minority Participation: America's Science and Technology Talent at the Crossroads.* The National Academies Press, 2011, https://doi.org/10.17226/12984

Olivares-Donoso, R., and C. González. "Undergraduate Research or Research-Based Courses: Which Is Most Beneficial for Science Students?" *Research in Science Education*, vol. 49 no. 1, 2019, 91–107, https://doi.org/10.1007/s11165-017-9616-4

Robnett, R.D., et al. "Longitudinal Associations Among Undergraduates' Research Experience, Self-Efficacy, and Identity." *Journal of Research in Science Teaching*, vol. 52 no. 6, 2015, 847–867, https://doi.org/10.1002/tea.21221

Routledge Undergraduate Research Series—Book Series. Routledge & CRC Press, n.d., www.routledge.com/Routledge-Undergraduate-Research-Series/book-series/RURS?gclid=CjwKCAiAu9yqBhBmEiwAHTx5p76cnVxSvSOISrY8zwnBt8UsZC02nB-8K0dboM1qnT_P5qb5iIAD-BoCm-kQAvD_BwE. Accessed 26 January 2024.

Russell, C.B., and G.C. Weaver. "A Comparative Study of Traditional, Inquiry-Based, and Research-Based Laboratory Curricula: Impacts on Understanding of the Nature of Science." *Chemistry Education Research and Practice*, vol. 12 no. 1, 2011, 57–67, https://doi.org/10.1039/C1RP90008K

Stephens, N.M., et al. "Closing the Social-Class Achievement Gap: A Difference-Education Intervention Improves First-Generation Students' Academic Performance and All Students' College Transition." *Psychological Science*, vol. 25 no. 4, 2014, 943–953, https://doi.org/10.1177/0956797613518349

Thompson, J.J., and D. Jensen-Ryan. "Becoming a "Science Person": Faculty Recognition and the Development of Cultural Capital in the Context of Undergraduate Biology Research." *CBE—Life Sciences Education*, vol. 17 no. 4, 2018, ar62, https://doi.org/10.1187/cbe.17-11-0229

Wilbur, T.G., and V.J. Roscigno. "First-Generation Disadvantage and College Enrollment/Completion." *Socius*, vol. 2, 2016, https://doi.org/10.1177/2378023116664351

2 So you want to start an undergraduate research office?

As evidence continues to grow supporting the benefits of high-impact practices like undergraduate research, scholarship, and creative activity (URSCA), faculty, staff, and administrators across the country are increasingly considering establishing formal undergraduate research offices.[1] If you are thinking about establishing such an office, we applaud your decision – and provide here an overview of issues and strategies to consider as you plan and develop your program. This chapter will walk you through the process of developing an initial concept, mission, and vision for a new URSCA office or center, paying particular attention to the task of determining the best context for launching the office within the existing structures on your campus.

Getting started

In our experience, there are a few standard ways in which URSCA offices generally have come to be:

- A faculty person identifies the need for expanded research opportunities and launches a small research program of their own, often funded by an individual research grant. The program grows over time, eventually serving more students and garnering campus support.
- An administrator (Dean or Provost) envisions the need for expanded research opportunities on their campus and enlists a faculty person to develop an office or a center, either within a school or division or as a cross-campus enterprise.[2]
- Several faculty or departments have already launched small grant-funded research programs and they, or a campus administrator, see the utility in supporting them administratively and coordinating certain activities under the broader umbrella of a campus URSCA office. This office can also offer services to others across campus not affiliated with the core-funded programs.

DOI: 10.4324/9781003154952-2

Whatever the case on your campus, it is important to begin with a clear assessment of what you are hoping to accomplish and how you expect to get there. The first questions you should ask yourself include: What need have I/my team/my administration identified that we believe can be met by providing students with undergraduate research, scholarship, and creativity/URSCA opportunities? Is it important that your campus develop a formal URSCA office to meet that need, or are there other mechanisms you should be considering? In what ways do students already engage in mentored research on your campus? Is there a culture of faculty individually mentoring students for independent study credit? Do you have an honors program, and how do its mission and requirements align with your vision? Do any departments offer seminars or courses that might provide good models for integrating undergraduate research into the classroom? Are there grant-funded programs or initiatives already in existence on your campus that offer mentored undergraduate research experiences (McNair, LSAMP, NSF, NIH-funded, etc.), and how will your office function in relation to them? Are there effective strategies and infrastructure already in place on campus for recruiting a diverse group of students in co-curricular activities such as URSCA?

The goal of this assessment is to get a clear picture of what your campus needs, and how a formal URSCA office might meet that need. In the middle of this chapter, we include a simple template and instructions for utilizing a logic model to help you think through the questions we pose, as well as others that are sure to arise. Once you have a clear understanding of these foundational questions, it will be much easier to develop an effective mission for your center, and a shared vision for what you aim to accomplish and what you will need in order to do so. Doing this preliminary work will help you assess the kinds of resources you have at your disposal and identify what you will need in order to launch your new center and communicate that vision to your campus partners, and eventually to the students you will serve. Launching such an ambitious project will inevitably involve diplomacy and some savvy political maneuvering – but if it is the right thing and the right time for your campus, you'll find allies who are keen to help you build something spectacular – and sustainable.

Where does your center fit within the campus administrative structure?

One of the most important things to think about is the question of the best institutional home for your center. Will you get the most support from a Dean, Provost, or Vice-Chancellor? We cannot stress enough the importance of affiliating with decision-makers who understand the importance of investing in the infrastructure required to support undergraduate research – they will be your greatest champions as your center grows.

If you are planning on serving only students within a particular discipline or division (STEM, Humanities, Social Sciences, e.g.), it might make the most sense to have a discussion with the appropriate Dean about divisional support and where the best place would be for your office to exist within their administrative structure. There are other important questions to ask as well: Will the director report to the Academic Dean, the Dean/Associate Dean of Student Success, or elsewhere? What fiscal and administrative support might you receive depending on where you sit within the division? How much autonomy will you, as director, have in continuing to shape the vision of the center? How does your vision align with the Dean/Division's? If you are envisioning a center that supports students from across campus and disciplines, it will make more sense for you to report to a Provost or Vice-Chancellor. This will give you access to multiple divisions and ensure support for your cross-campus work.

We find it is easiest to envision how these questions might play out in practice by looking at real-world examples. At one of our campuses (CSU Monterey Bay), a founding faculty member in the College of Science was concerned about our students' low graduation and graduate school acceptance rates. Having had some success in obtaining grants that supported undergraduate research in STEM, with a focus on students historically underserved in higher education, he was instrumental in launching our campus' McNair Scholars program (funded in 2007 by the US Department of Education), which became the foundation for a growing, centralized, and interdisciplinary Undergraduate Research Opportunities Center (UROC). While UROC has grown exponentially since its formal inception in 2009 as a cross-campus center, its vision and mission remain linked to that original objective of supporting student academic success, particularly for students underrepresented in higher education; a mission that also aligns us with our campus's founding vision and current academic plan. At the time of the center's official incorporation, the campus was also building a library. Then-Director William Head worked with campus leadership to situate the center in the new building, alongside other key student support services including the writing program, the first-year seminar program, the tutoring center, and the counseling office. The reporting line also moved from the science Dean's office to the campus Provost, who was in the best position to support the center's work across the various schools and divisions that made up the university. You can read a detailed account of how UROC and other URSCA programs determined their place within a variety of campus structures in the 2012 Council on Undergraduate Research publication *Undergraduate Research Offices & Programs: Models & Practices*, also available for download from the UROC website.[3]

The right place at the right time

Before going too far down the road, it's important to read the lay of the land. Particular attention should be given to determining the best context for launching an undergraduate research office/center within the existing structures of the campus. Should your office be a stand-alone unit, or should it be embedded in other existing student support services on campus? For instance, you may gain more traction with an undergraduate research program that is part of a suite of high-impact practices (HIPs) such as service learning, supplemental instruction, and/or writing programs, if this is an area your campus is already committed to supporting. If you are on a two-year campus, it may be especially important to connect with existing articulation agreements/partnerships with regional research-focused four-year colleges and universities. At California State University, Monterey Bay (CSUMB), we have had success recently in procuring grant funding jointly with regional community college partners in order to support their students engaging in summer research engagement with faculty at our four-year institution. It's worth exploring options to create and codify relationships with regional partners in this way (see the vignette in this chapter from Valencia College).

In addition to thinking through how your center will align with other campus programs, you should also consider how the timing of creating an URSCA center can align with other initiatives. Can your center build off of a current grant initiative, strategic plan, or new mission of the college or university? As the benefits of engaging in undergraduate research are disproportionately beneficial to students of traditionally underrepresented ethnicities and students who are the first generation in their family in college, it's important to consider issues of equity and inclusion in your strategic planning. Most campuses now have dedicated equity and inclusion units, and developing programs in collaboration with them will ensure close alignment with the goals and values of the campus with respect to access and broad participation in both curricular and co-curricular programs. In thinking about recruiting a diverse array of student participants, a good place to start is with student support offices on campus. If your campus has any TRIO programs (including McNair), a Louis Stokes Alliance for Minority Participation (LSAMP) office, or other offices specializing in student support/scaffolding, they can be important allies/resources. At CSUMB, we have been able to leverage our participation in the statewide CSU-LSAMP alliance to bolster our professional preparation for undergraduate research participants.

Overall, aligning the development or growth of your center with the momentum of other campus initiatives can help build the initial investment and may inform whether the center is embedded in another program (e.g., a college or honors program) or a stand-alone campus center.

The right message, the right audience

If your office is going to serve a wide disciplinary range of students/majors, it will be important to create opportunities to directly interact with administrators, faculty, and students in the pertinent academic units. Because research is important to faculty retention, tenure, and promotion – even in universities and colleges where teaching is the primary focus – it's important to work with administrative leadership to ensure alignment of values and goals. In particular, it's essential to work with Deans/Associate Deans to ensure that faculty engagement in undergraduate research in each academic unit you serve is an important and recognized component of the tenure and promotion process. The same message can be conveyed to faculty; at primarily undergraduate institutions, conducting research with undergraduates can be an effective and important strategy for faculty to be stellar researchers and teachers.[4] In our experience, some faculty may be skeptical, citing the extra work and potentially lower prestige products involved in mentoring undergraduates in the research realm. Anticipating such reluctance is a compelling reason to have clear and open discussions with faculty about tenure/promotion expectations up front, emphasizing the potentially rich interplay between teaching, research mentoring, and furthering their own research. This is also an opportunity to encourage faculty (especially junior faculty on the tenure track) to think deeply about a long-term plan for engaging undergraduates in research as a successful "survival" strategy starting in the early part of their career.[5] The same approach can be used in conversations with lecturers/contingent faculty (non-tenure-track), though the intersection of institutional expectations and career aspirations are of course nuances that will vary individually.

Finally, it is imperative to procure the support of your upper administration. Having a Provost and/or President that is highly supportive – and vocal about their support – is invaluable. Not only does it highlight the good work that you are doing, and encourage the participation of faculty and staff from around campus, but it also provides a natural means for leveraging the existence of your new center to procure more operational funds for student research activities. The chances of procuring external grants (either for federal monies or for private donors/foundations) are bolstered considerably when it's clear that the campus administration is fully supportive of your initiatives. Most upper-level administrators who are paying close attention to campus vision and successes will naturally lend their support if it's the right time/right context (see the first paragraph of this chapter!) – but occasionally, it will be important to get an audience with them and remind them. For those considering creating an office of undergraduate research, it is critical to answer two fundamental questions: how do you communicate the role of your office and how do you fund it?

Financial support

Starting an undergraduate research center will naturally require resources, some of which can be provided as "sweat equity" by keen and committed faculty and staff, but most of which will require additional financial resources. Whether you are starting with a faculty member who is given a supplemental administrative allowance and a one-room office, or you are starting with a large centralized suite of offices replete with a full staff, funding – and the sustainability of that funding – will, of course, play an outsized role as you consider the range and nature of support you'll be able to provide to undergraduates participating in research. Chapter 5 will provide further strategies for funding an URSCA office.

Exercise: logic model for program building

A logic model can be very useful as a kind of working document to organize your thoughts about different aspects of your research center. Furthermore, a logic model can be used to explain or demonstrate to others your center's role in the overall campus scheme, whom it serves, and how it aligns with your campus strategic plan/mission. Here we invite you to develop your own logic model as a planning exercise. We'll be using a standard logic model template, which we ask you to fill out according to the descriptions listed below (note that we recommend doing this "out of order," working on your problem statement(s) and outcomes before moving on to the rest of the segments).

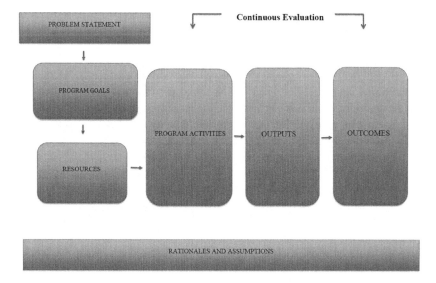

Figure 2.1 Logic model template.

Problem statement

Start things off by defining the "problem" – that is, the issue or issues that you see the need to address, ideally through the lens of student success. These may focus on questions of academic achievement, the development of transferable skills (critical thinking, oral and written communication, technical skills, information literacy, etc.), student sense of belonging on campus, career readiness, or rates of matriculation to graduate programs. Try to describe why the issue(s) are urgent for your campus and require immediate attention – and, if possible, align them/put them in the context of campus strategic plans. There may be several problems your team identifies. Putting them into the context of the logic model will help you determine which can/should be addressed by your center (and how), which might be best addressed in partnership with other campus support services, and which might need to be addressed elsewhere on campus. At this point, it is important to have developed a clear understanding of the literature addressing barriers to student success, as well as barriers to participation in URSCA. Understanding common barriers and how they play out on your campus through a close examination of institutional data is key to the success of this exercise. While the data paint only a portion of the picture, there are usually some fairly clear problem areas you will be able to identify. For example, if your demographics show that among your campus population graduation rates for one particular group (e.g., ethnicity, gender, and returning or transfer students) are lower than for others, you have identified one problem your office may be able to address. In addition to working with your institutional data, we encourage you to have deep conversations across campus in order to develop a nuanced picture of the student success issues at your college or university.

Defining goals

As the name suggests, here you will want to provide a succinct list of project goals, relating them directly to the problem statement(s) you have developed. For example, an academic achievement problem/goal pairing might address the issue of STEM students stopping out, or transferring out of a major, at a key time (usually end of sophomore year). Your goal could be to reduce the attrition by 15–25% over a set number of years. Another problem/goal pairing might address a particular barrier to certain groups of students participating in URSCA. If your data show that you have extremely low participation rates for, say, African American students, your goal could be to increase the number of African American students participating in URSCA each year from 1% of enrolled African American students to 5%.

Resources/inputs

Here you should list any and all resources that will be available for your initiative – this might include personnel, funding sources, space, and campus or regional partnerships. In your startup phase, pay special attention to places on campus where you may be able to leverage shared resources. In practice, this might look like negotiating a small percentage of an already-employed staff person's time for a set number of years to assist with the nuts and bolts of running the office. And don't forget about material resources: for example, we understand most URSCA programs teach students about poster preparation and encourage or require them to present a poster at a local, regional, or national conference. Are there any programs on campus that already own a poster printer that your program might be able to utilize until you are in a position to purchase your own? Is there a print shop locally that would offer reduced rates to your students, etc.? In terms of partnerships, we encourage you to think broadly about the resources in your area; we have found that at small/less research-intensive campuses, important partnerships can be formed with regional research institutions to vastly expand the opportunities available to your students. At CSUMB, for example, we formed partnerships affording our students the opportunity to undertake mentored research experiences with faculty and graduate students at the Monterey Bay Aquarium Research Institute (MBARI), Moss Landing Marine Labs (MLML), and Stanford's Hopkins Marine Station, among others. Your resources might also include your local museums and historical societies, faculty with active research enterprises or labs, underutilized spaces on campus, the potential to access student fees to help fund your work, campus funding sources to potentially support student research, etc. We encourage you to dig deeply and think creatively about what your potential resources might be.

Activities

Here you should describe the principal activities that comprise your program/initiative. Some of these will be standard URSCA office practices like workshops (see Chapter 6 for examples), and connecting students to mentored URSCA experiences both on- and off-campus. Other activities should be directly connected to the problem/goal pairings that anchor the first sections of your logic model. The academic achievement example we gave of STEM students stopping out, or transferring out of a major at a key time, for which you've established a goal to reduce the attrition by a certain percent, can be addressed by a plethora of activities. Familiarizing yourself with the literature will give you a clear understanding of current best practices for addressing problems such as this that are likely to occur widely. From there, you can design activities suited to your campus, and to the resources and people you have to work with. You might decide to address this issue by introducing a short freshman research experience designed with the goal of early engagement with the major and to build critical relationships with tenure-track faculty whom students might not be able to otherwise meet until later in their academic careers, two key factors in addressing retention among beginning students.

Outputs

This should be a list of outputs from your program activities – in other words, the product(s) of each of your activities, or what you are going to do and who you are going to reach. Note that these should be tangible, measurable results stemming directly from the activities; they will form the basis of your desired outcomes. If we are to continue on with or same example from the previous sections, your outputs over a set number of years would include actually doing the freshman research experience each year, the number of students you expect to participate in the activity, the number of faculty the students will connect with, as well as any additional measurables you may want to build into the activity. Mapping your outputs before you begin your endeavor will also prepare you for a successful assessment of your program down the line.

Outcomes

Following from the outputs, outcomes are things that you predict will occur as a result of your program being implemented. Note that this should include both short- and long-term outcomes, capturing the changes that will ensue from the implementation of your program. A critical element of this is some measure of how your program will affect systematic change in your campus community. Ultimately your outcomes will paint a picture of the impact you expect to have. We have found that thinking about the entire process we are laying out as a series of if–then relationships has helped us come up with tangible yet effective and sometimes even visionary outcomes. If all of our students were given the opportunity to engage in [insert activity], what shifts in student achievement would we likely see over three to five years, and ultimately what culture change might we expect to see on our campus over time? **We actually recommend making this the second section you work on as you fill in your logic model.** This will allow you to identify your problems and dream big about the culture change you would like to see happen to shift or change those conditions. You can use the middle sections (resources, activities, and outputs) to bring your ideas back to the more practical and pragmatic concerns of how to achieve your goals.

Finally, underlying all of your working elements are your *Rationales* and *Assumptions*. Rationale should be supported by arguments based on research, best practices, and your own experience in order to describe how the change you intend to bring about will happen. Assumptions, of course, are any and all conditions that are necessary and sufficient to pull off a successful program.

Whether you're starting small with a one- or two-person office, or developing a full-blown center for URSCA, you'll want to carefully consider a number of contextual and logistical issues before you commence operations. Your first steps will involve the challenge of balancing resource availability, campus mission/goals/demographics, administrative, staff, and faculty support, and wide-ranging expectations across campus. And you'll want to be clear about what you're trying to achieve – that is, what campus problem(s) are you trying to solve? With all of these things in mind, you'll be ready to lay the groundwork for your new office/center – and take the next steps toward planning staff and structure (more on that in the next chapter).

VIGNETTE 2.1   The Valencia community college program on research and transfer

Melonie W. Sexton, Ph.D., Undergraduate Research Coordinator, DTC & WPC Social Science Coordinator, Professor of Psychological Sciences, Valencia College, Orlando, Florida

History of undergraduate research at Valencia

Many two-year institutions pride themselves on creating exemplary experiences for students inside the classroom. The focus at these schools is typically on teaching and learning. The philosophy of most open-access institutions is that anyone who is committed to learning can be successful when provided with the right resources. In 2015, a group of faculty at Valencia College identified a gap in the educational curriculum at the college: access to engage in undergraduate research. Students who were interested in gaining research experience early in their academic experience did not have a clear pathway to do so. Additionally, a handful of faculty members were creating curriculum that encompassed undergraduate research; however, there was no guidance or documentation of this work being done at the college. By 2018, Dr. Melonie Sexton was appointed as

Valencia's college-wide Undergraduate Research Coordinator and charged with addressing this issue. She, along with a small group of faculty and administrators, formed an undergraduate research board with the purpose of developing a more defined undergraduate research program. To truly make research more accessible for our students, Dr. Sexton began to focus on building relationships with the University of Central Florida (UCF), specifically the Office of Undergraduate Research (OUR) and the Academic Advancement Programs (AAPs). Given that 80% of all Valencia students transfer to UCF, she knew that creating this academic bridge was going to be a vital part of the program's success.

By establishing a strong relationship between partner schools, UCF and Valencia have developed a rich biome of significant research experiences. This partnership has led to collaborative workshops, mentorship, persistence among students, and, most importantly, transferable research skills.

UCF's intentions/outcome

The University of Central Florida's OUR and AAPs are committed to promoting the success of transfer students through undergraduate research and graduate school preparation. Given the limited time that transfer students have at UCF, especially in light of the focus on two-year graduation, both offices understand the crucial importance of outreaching to students before they transfer so they can fully take advantage of the opportunities available. The partnership between these UCF offices and Undergraduate Research at Valencia has led to a pipeline of students who come to UCF prepared to engage in research-focused initiatives. Importantly, because of these collaborations, students are also transferring with built-in networks at UCF that serve to provide them with support and community from their first day at UCF.

Valencia students who participate in the collaborations between OUR, AAP, and Valencia Undergraduate Research are invited to apply to programs including the Summer Research Academy, T-LEARN Learning Community, the Research and Mentoring Program, and the McNair Scholars Program. These programs are strong pipelines to success at UCF, where students are provided with resources to connect to research, funded, and supported through graduation.

Each collaborative event between Valencia Undergraduate Research, OUR, and AAP leads students to connect to supportive staff, learn about resources that will impact their future, and gain important information about what steps they can take toward success. It also demystifies the transfer experience as they are able to hear from transfer students who have successfully navigated their journey from state college to UCF.

Outreach and collaboration efforts

Workshops

One of the most successful cornerstones of this partnership has been the ongoing undergraduate research workshop series. What began as face-to-face seminars at the joint downtown campus, quickly evolved into online virtual sessions open to students from both institutions and from every campus. Since beginning our shared workshops series, we have seen over 400 students attend these information sessions. Topics covered include "What is Undergraduate Research?," "How to get started in Undergraduate Research," and "Honors Undergraduate Research: transitioning from Seneff into Burnett." Each semester, we schedule a minimum of four workshops (typically offering one workshop a month). These programmatic events are integral for students who are just learning about undergraduate research and are interested in networking with fellow scholars and academic directors.

Bi-annual showcase

When developing the undergraduate research program at Valencia, the advisory board knew that one of the requirements to a successful program would be to create opportunities for students to disseminate their work to the public. Although some of this work was happening in small pockets throughout the college, the advisory board tasked the coordinator with the responsibility of creating a bi-annual, college-wide research poster showcase. Since its inception in 2017, the showcase has grown into a major event. The purpose of the event is to provide students a forum to present their research to the academic community. Oftentimes, our students have never presented in a conference setting, so the showcase at Valencia is touted as low-stakes and encourages students to attend to practice their networking and presentation skills.

Over the years, the showcase has attracted not only more students but also more participants from the Orlando community. The partnership between Valencia and UCF is especially important here. Each term, we ask several research administrators and faculty to act as judges for the showcase. As a result, there has been an increase in Valencia students who have applied for, and been accepted into, multiple research programs at UCF. Valencia students are now intentionally applying for Summer Research Experience for Undergraduates (REUs) at UCF, the Summer Research Academy (SRA), the Ronald E. McNair Post-Baccalaureate Achievement Program, the Research and Mentoring Program (RAMP), and Introduction to Research & Creative Scholarship Opportunities (INTROs), just to name a few.

Campus visits

Another practice that has been added as an emblem of this transfer pathway is the summer visitation program. Each summer, Valencia's Undergraduate Research and Honors Program coordinates with the directors of the Academic Advancement Program and Office of Undergraduate Research to create an all-day visitation for Valencia students planning to transfer to UCF.

By working closely with the Academic Advancement Program and the Office of Undergraduate Research, Dr. Sexton has developed an experience tailored to the needs of transfer students. During their trip, the students speak with advisors in the transfer center, learn about scholarship opportunities, and take a tour of the campus. The highlight of the trip, however, is when students get to visit actual research laboratories. For one hour, students speak directly to principal investigators and graduate students and discuss the projects that are currently being conducted in the labs.

Notes

1 Kinzie, J., et al. "Promoting Persistence and Success of Underrepresented Students: Lessons for Teaching and Learning." *New Directions for Teaching and Learning*, vol. 2008 no. 115, 2008, 21–38, https://doi.org/10.1002/tl.323

2 The question of whether to develop an office or center is one we suggest you address. What kind of unit does your campus need in order to facilitate URSCA? The difference between an "office" and a "center" can vary from campus to campus, so it's worth considering what these terms mean on your campus. In some universities, the term "center" is associated primarily with grant-funded research programs, with little or no expectation of campus support. An office, in contrast, may connote staff support from the campus – but at the same time may make it more difficult to procure a campus commitment to resources to get things off the ground as a consequence.

3 Head, W. and J. Brown. "California State University, Monterey Bay: Undergraduate Research Opportunities Center." *Undergraduate Research Offices & Programs: Models & Practices*. Edited by J. Kinkead and L. Blockus, Council on Undergraduate Research, 2012, pp. 95–122, https://csumb.edu/media/csumb/section-editors/undergraduate-research-opportunities-center/st-block-103–1463520336770-raw-stblock371439423224397rawstblock-111427908330759rawchaptersixuroc2012.pdf

4 Banks, J.E., et al. 2018. "Alliance for Change: Broadening Participation in Undergraduate Research at California State University." *Scholarship and Practice of Undergraduate Research*, vol. 1 no. 4, 2018, 5–11.
5 Eagan, M.K., Jr. "Engaging Undergraduates in Science Research: Not Just About Faculty Willingness." *Research in Higher Education*, vol. 52 no. 2, 2011, 151–177.

References

Banks, J.E., et al. "Alliance for Change: Broadening Participation in Undergraduate Research at California State University." *Scholarship and Practice of Undergraduate Research (SPUR)*, vol. 1 no. 4, 2018, 5–11.

Eagan, M.K., Jr., et al. "Engaging Undergraduates in Science Research: Not Just About Faculty Willingness." *Research in Higher Education*, vol. 52 no. 2, 2011, 151–177.

Head, W., and J. Brown. "California State University, Monterey Bay: Undergraduate Research Opportunities Center." *Undergraduate Research Offices & Programs: Models & Practices*. Edited by J. Kinkead and L. Blockus, Council on Undergraduate Research, 2012, pp. 95–122, https://csumb.edu/media/csumb/section-editors/undergraduate-research-opportunities-center/st-block-103-1463520336770-raw-stblock-371439423224397rawstblock111427908330759rawchaptersixuroc2012.pdf

Kinzie, J., et al. "Promoting Persistence and Success of Underrepresented Students: Lessons for Teaching and Learning." *New Directions for Teaching and Learning*, vol. 2008 no. 115, 2008, 21–38, https://doi.org//10.1002/tl.323

3   Staffing and office structure

In prior chapters, we considered the benefits of undergraduate research – for students, their mentors, and the campus as a whole, and discussed the importance of carefully considering your office's purpose and goals. In this chapter, we'll turn our focus to more fundamental questions surrounding the nuts and bolts of establishing and running an office, offering advice on what you will need to think about in order to get your enterprise off the ground. We will explore resource and infrastructure needs, offer some guideposts for strategic planning, and present a series of case studies that illustrate different successful approaches.

Setting the groundwork: faculty administrative time

In our experience, most offices of undergraduate research, scholarship, and creative activity (URSCA) began with the enthusiasm – and labor – of a single faculty person. Whether that faculty member started by incorporating undergraduate research into a large federal grant, was asked to develop an office by a Dean or Provost, or saw the need to support and connect a variety of unrelated research and mentoring programs across campus, generally the first years of an office or a center's development are led by a crew of one. If this person is you – congratulations! You have work to do, and a great opportunity to shape a well-thought-out program for your campus.

As the chief cook and bottle-washer for your newly formed office, it will be important to start by mapping out the amount of time you can reasonably be expected to devote to this work, both during the academic year and during the summer, as well as the type of compensation you will receive. It is common for a campus to offer course release as well as a small research stipend to an incoming faculty director; how much time is offered will directly correspond to how carefully and efficiently a program can be established and managed.

Any discussion of faculty time should also include a plan for institutional growth. The more your office grows, the more students that are

DOI: 10.4324/9781003154952-3

served, the more deeply ingrained you become in the fabric of campus – the more time you will need to devote to it. As faculty director, you should have ongoing discussions with your campus administration or supporting unit to help both of you plan for the expanded amount of administrative time you will devote to managing a growing program. This might look like a plan to gradually increase your administrative time to anywhere from 50% to 100% of your effort, as well as a plan for creating and sustaining additional administrative positions.

For a faculty director, there are additional issues to consider: you will need to be sure that your work as director meets departmental service obligations and is recognized as such by the appropriate academic personnel committees when it comes time to evaluate you for merit and promotion (these issues will be discussed in more depth in Chapter 8). You should also think about how your office will operate in summer. Most faculty are off contract at that time – how much work is expected, and how will that be compensated? If you are developing a program that focuses primarily on providing on-campus research experiences during the academic year, you might expect to spend very little of your summer time in the office. However, if your program will also incorporate summer research experiences on or off-campus, and the professional development seminars or workshops these programs normally offer, your summer commitment could look more like a full-time job. Chapter 5 of this book offers more insight into finding funding to support these kinds of programmatic needs as your office grows.

The importance of an advisory board

As is the case when developing any major program or initiative, it is important not to go it alone. You may already have collaborators in your department, across campus, or in your administration who are willing and eager to help you think through the development of your undergraduate research office. However, forming an advisory board can help cement those relationships and ensure that you are receiving the support you need. Advisory board members, carefully chosen, can be valuable thought partners and advocates and also help ensure support for – and recognition of – your program across campus. As your office expands, they can also help with various activities ranging from adjudicating awards, to leading workshops, or even serving as student research mentors.

Generally, advisory boards are drawn from the faculty of the departments your program will serve, but it is often politically astute to invite other key administrators to join. Engaging them in your work will help make them champions of your program. A manageable size in the early years of your office might be between five and seven people. We have also seen advisory boards at larger campuses that comprise as many as 20 people. In most cases, board or committee members serve in staggered three-year terms, thus ensuring some continuity within your group. We have also found it a good practice to have a Dean or other senior administrator appoint members to the board on your behalf, and at your recommendation. This signals administrative support for both your work and theirs.

Faculty and research mentors

The key factor in developing and sustaining undergraduate research activities is your faculty. If you are part of a larger research campus, you may also have graduate students and professional research staff whom you can add to your list of potential mentors. If you are developing your campus' first URSCA office, be sure not to start by trying to reinvent the wheel – chances are, many of your faculty are already mentoring students on their own in one way or another. One of your first tasks should be to assess who is doing this work, and what they are working to achieve. Are they looking for more assistance in a lab? Are they participating because they have a commitment to student success? Are they engaged in discussions about high-impact practices? Are they continuing to work with a small group of students who took a class and wanted to dig deeper into a topic? Understanding their motivation will help you create a program that meets the needs of your campus. You should also assess whether those faculty already mentoring students intend to make it part of their practice going forward, and if they can support more students – which is especially likely in the case of science faculty whose labs can accommodate more than a single researcher. Next, assess how your office can add value to the good work already happening, as well as increase opportunities for students to connect to faculty and research opportunities.

Large campuses may want to take advantage of mentor-matching services in order to accommodate the sheer number of people at their institutions. Services like the *Mentorcollective* platform are designed specifically for institutions that want to "deploy structured mentoring programs at scale."[1]

Smaller institutions often do not have the need for, or resources to pay for, these kinds of services, but instead opt to create programs tailored to the specific needs of their campus. The undergraduate research program at Princeton, for example, has developed an opt-in program called ReMatch that connects undergraduate students to graduate students and postdoctoral researchers and is designed to "provide undergraduates with early hands-on opportunities to ignite and sustain their interest in research" and prepare them for more independent work in later years.[2] The University of Michigan's Undergraduate Research Opportunity Program, much like our own at California State University, Monterey Bay, has developed a formal process for accepting applications for mentor-led research projects and connecting students to those opportunities.[3] In each of these cases, our larger staffing structure allows us to help support the mentor–mentee relationships once a match is made, as well as offer important professional development support to the students doing the research, easing the burden on the faculty to do all things.

However, it does not take a large staff to foster and support good mentor–mentee relationships. If your office will not immediately have the capacity to engage at this level, there are many good resources for mentor training that you can point your faculty to. We will discuss this more in Chapter 7: Facilitating the mentor–mentee relationship.

Physical space

In our experience, it is very important to have a physical space that students can identify as the URSCA office. This is especially important if you wish to connect with students who might not naturally go out and find research opportunities on their own. You are here to help them navigate the university research structure, and they need to be able to find you. However, not every office or program will open its doors with an allocation of space of their own. Thus, it is important to think about other entities on campus with which you might at first affiliate in order to share some basic resources and get yourself out in front of students.

Think about what resources you need in terms of physical space, computing, Internet, website, printing, basic office support, as well as other items related to the mission you have crafted. Are there other offices on campus with which you share some basic academic or student success goals? Would they be willing to share space, resources, or co-host events with you, and what synergies might such an arrangement support? Also to consider: are there specific spaces on campus that students will be most likely to find you? One of the key challenges faculty directors of small offices have identified is the difficulty of operating out of their personal faculty offices: students from outside your own department may have difficulty finding you; and when the directorship rotates to a new faculty person (as is often the case), the location of the URSCA office changes as well, making finding the office even more difficult.

Our own office, the Undergraduate Research Opportunities Center (UROC) at CSU Monterey Bay, began when our campus was quite young and still developing its physical plan. Our first offices were in a repurposed military barrack on the far outskirts of campus. We had a dedicated office space but it was not ideal. When our campus set out to build a new university library, which was to serve as the student hub of campus and include the offices for advising, tutoring, and the writing program, we jumped at the opportunity to share space with the latter two programs in a second story wing of the building. Due to the support of a Provost who believed in the importance of undergraduate research, we now have a space that has proved to be extremely advantageous in its centrality, allowing us to reach out to almost every student who comes to campus.

Staffing: planning strategically for growth and sustainability

Most established offices are eventually served by a larger staff, ranging from a full-time director/administrative support team to much larger groups that include professional academic positions who directly oversee various ancillary programs. As you read through the subsequent chapters, you will be presented with various programmatic structures made possible by these additional positions.

Your staffing should always be linked to the programmatic activities you identify as central to the mission of your office. Understanding what kind of support you will want to provide to students, as well as what kinds of campus events your office will host will help you come up with an appropriate staffing plan. You should think not only about what is possible in the start-up phase but also about what support you would like to offer within a five- or ten-year period. As we will describe later, our own Undergraduate Research Opportunity Center staff grew as our mission shifted from administration of a small, boutique undergraduate research program, to a campus resource center with the goal of providing access to all students. A good way to develop an understanding of what staff you might need is to make a list of the things you can do, and things staff can do more efficiently. The worksheet at the end of this chapter is intended to help you think through these issues, but we offer a few ideas later.

Often it is more efficient for staff to handle student support functions such as travel, research placements, stipends, add/drop codes (if research is undertaken for credit), and grant administration. Faculty time might be better spent offering workshops, seminars, and other research curriculum. As offices grow, there are often additional programs and services they develop, including support programs for faculty mentors, peer mentoring programs, campus research symposia and events, outreach to new constituencies, and of course assessment of the impact of their work. A quick look at the staffing structures of other offices and centers can help you think about what you might need as you develop.

The organizational chart below represents the California State University, Monterey Bay UROC office at the point that we had the most robust staffing plan in place. Over the course of five years, our program grew from a full-time, grant-funded faculty director position, supported by a staff assistant director, to an office of ten full-time professional staff, six of whom were permanently funded by the university. The remaining four positions were grant-funded, with conversations underway with campus administration about how to make those permanent. We also created a number of student positions that let us expand our services, outreach, and assessment and helped with the administrative workload of a growing office.

UROC manages a number of student support grants, including our McNair Scholars and Louis Stokes Alliance for Minority Participation (LSAMP) programs, as well as others funded by large federal programs. As we have noted elsewhere,

> UROC's robust services and hand-on approach require a considerable amount of supervision, oversight, and coordination by UROC staff members. Further, given that our small campus lacks [other] traditional offices that support . . . students [doing undergraduate research], UROC staff members assume additional responsibilities that would typically fall under the purview of honors colleges or fellowship offices.[4]

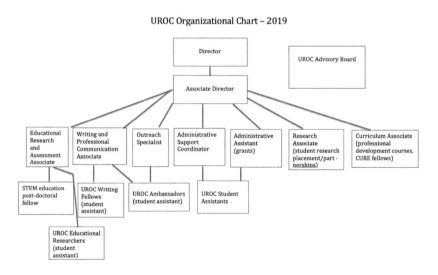

Figure 3.1 UROC organizational chart 2019.

Led by a pair of full-time staff directors, one with a Ph.D. in the Sciences and the other with a Ph.D. in the Humanities, our team includes the following: a Research Associate who oversees student research experience placement and mentor recruitment both on- and off-campus; a Curriculum Associate who teaches a two-year professional development curriculum, which is also offered as a series of open workshops, and who co-administers our CURE fellows faculty development program; our Writing and Professional Communication Associate works closely with students on research communication, leads a peer-to-peer writing program, and serves as the de facto fellowship advisor for campus; the Educational Research and Assessment Associate oversees the assessment of all of our grants and programs with the goal of knowledge generation and program improvement; and our Outreach Specialist connects CSUMB students to our programs, and manages student outreach to community colleges and local high schools. Two administrative support positions oversee all center and grant-related operations; and a STEM education postdoctoral fellow works closely with our staff, with a special emphasis on understanding the impact of the CURE fellows program.

The vignettes that close out this chapter present a variety of other programmatic and staffing scenarios for you to consider as you build out your program.

Building infrastructure

The Council on Undergraduate Research is an invaluable resource for all things, but one publication in particular can help you consider how your existing campus research infrastructure can support your short- and long-term programmatic needs and goals. *Characteristics of Excellence in Undergraduate Research (COEUR)* is "a summary of best practices that support and sustain highly effective undergraduate research environments."[5] In addition to several short essays that describe how various campuses have utilized the framework, it presents a highly detailed outline of the various elements of a campus infrastructure that, if properly developed, should serve to support the undergraduate research enterprise.[6] Any faculty member or team tasked with setting up an URSCA office should sit down with this list and consider what infrastructure their campus currently has to support their mission, as well as what areas are in need of development in order for them to reach their academic and student support goals. For campuses with some resources to devote to intentionally building a new program, or expanding an existing one, we also highly recommend gathering a team to attend the Council on Undergraduate Research's *Initiating and Sustaining Undergraduate Research Programs*

Institute. Further information on the CUR institutes can be found at: www.cur.org/what/events/institutes/isurp/

Summary

There are a variety of ways of administering an office of undergraduate research, scholarship, and creative activity. Most offices begin with a staff of one part-time faculty director who receives release from teaching and a small stipend to begin the work. While small enterprises can be supported by graduate or undergraduate student assistants, as offices grow and begin to offer more comprehensive programmatic services, additional staff positions will be needed. Plan strategically for growth, being sure to secure commitments of university resources as you scale up your operations.

VIGNETTE 3.1

John Celenza, Boston University, Undergraduate
Research Opportunities Program (UROP)

Introduction

Boston University's Undergraduate Research Opportunities Program (UROP) facilitates the participation of Boston University undergraduate students in faculty-mentored research and scholarship across all disciplines. UROP's mission is to nurture curiosity, to capture imagination, and to cultivate relationships between faculty and students beyond the classroom to shape independent, innovative, and collaborative leaders. UROP helps students identify and connect with faculty members who want to involve undergraduates in their research and provides financial support for summer and academic year stipends, research supplies, and travel for research and to professional meetings. Funding from UROP's budget is awarded based on competitive application submissions, and UROP also seeks and manages external funding to support undergraduate research.

Leadership and office structure

UROP is under the office of the Provost and has a leadership team of a Director (part-time effort from a faculty member), an Assistant Director (full-time staff member), and Program Administrator (full-time staff member). The leadership team determines the overall direction of the program and all members participate in outreach and recruiting activities. The Assistant Director and Program Administrator also manage the UROP application process and organize events such as the annual UROP Symposium, weekly summer workshops, and targeted information sessions throughout the year. In addition, the Assistant Director and Program Administrator manage the financial aspects of the program. UROP has a two-room office on campus where the Assistant Director and Program Administrator work. During the past ten years, UROP applications have increased by >60% with an even greater increase in funds awarded due to increases in the minimum wage. To facilitate this increased student interest in UROP, the leadership has streamlined the application process using an online system through Jotform and always is looking for ways to make the application and award management process more efficient.

The UROP application process

Students identify research opportunities in four ways: (1) faculty members post opportunities on the UROP website; (2) students speak with their instructors or academic advisors; (3) students peruse faculty research interests on departmental websites; and (4) students meet with UROP staff to discuss their research interests. Once a student–mentor relationship has been initiated, students work with their faculty mentors to prepare and submit applications to UROP for funding. These applications describe research objectives, methods, and significance, and they are reviewed during three different competitive funding cycles each year (fall, spring, and summer). UROP provides funding for: stipends, research supplies, and research- or conference-related travel. All stipend and supply proposals are reviewed by the UROP Faculty Advisory Committee, which determines the suitability of funding for each project. Travel applications are reviewed by the UROP staff and directors on a rolling basis. In a typical year, UROP funds over 600 applications awarding over $1,000,000.

UROP Faculty Advisory Committee

The UROP Faculty Advisory Committee (FAC) is comprised of faculty from disciplines across the university designed to mirror the diversity of applications received by UROP. The FAC reviews all student applications for research funding and decides funding priorities. Applicants benefit from knowing that their applications were reviewed by experts and report that the system appears fair. The FAC also advises the UROP director and staff on larger programmatic goals and policies and over the years changes to the application process and scope of funded awards have come from ideas initiated by the FAC. FAC members frequently are active themselves as undergraduate research mentors and typically serve on the FAC for at least three application cycles. While the FAC is uncompensated, recruitment of faculty for the FAC has not been an issue as many are motivated by their own positive research experiences as undergraduates.

VIGNETTE 3.2

Colin Shaw, Montana State University, Undergraduate
Scholars Program (USP)

Overview of undergraduate research at Montana State University

Montana State University (MSU) established early leadership in undergraduate research with the launch of the Undergraduate Scholars Program (USP) in the early 1990s. Today, MSU has an active undergraduate research enterprise facilitated by a loosely coordinated network of offices and programs that work together on a largely ad hoc basis. The decentralized system provides flexibility and allows space for innovation, but also engenders inefficiency and makes it difficult for students to navigate the complex landscape of research options. Grant-funded programs including the MSU McNair Scholars program, Montana INBRE (Idea Network of Biomedical Research Excellence), and Montana Space Grant Consortium (MSGC) as well as some internally funded disciplinary programs are administered by stand-alone offices reporting to different departments and colleges. As the largest multidisciplinary undergraduate research organization, however, USP still plays a central role in fostering cooperation between programs, though there is no formal administrative coordination. The long-standing ambition to develop a more intentional structure to steer the broader undergraduate research enterprise is slowly gaining ground against institutional inertia.

USP: The Undergraduate Scholars Program

In 1994, Provost Mark Emmert convened a committee to develop and launch a new campus-wide undergraduate research program.

Music Professor Greg Young was hired as a half-time director with a course-load reduction. The program was allocated 0.1 FTE for an administrative assistant shared with the Math/Science Resource Center and an operating budget of $30,000 provided by the Vice President for Research and the Provost. Matching funds were raised year to year from the colleges, departments, and sponsored research indirect cost accounts to supplement the student award budget. An annual student research celebration, building on a small event initiated by business professor David Snepenger in 1991, eventually grew into an annual showcase for upward of 250 student research, scholarly, and creative presentations.

As USP programs expanded, demand for staff resources and matching funds grew. A 0.5 FTE classified position was added in the early 2000s. In 2012, USP Director Colin Shaw secured general fund support for student awards and increased salary support for the Director (0.5 FTE) and Program Coordinator (1.0 FTE). A new First Year Research Experience (FYRE) program was initiated in 2014 and in 2016 MSU was chosen to host the next National Conference on Undergraduate Research (NCUR, 2020) and the Year of Undergraduate Research (YOUR).[7]

Over the past decade, core programs at USP have funded faculty-mentored undergraduate research projects, student conference travel including NCUR, a first-year research experience seminar, and the MSU Student Research Celebration from a general fund operations budget of nearly $250,000/year. Over the years, USP has administered several externally funded programs including three National Science Foundation (NSF) Research Experiences for Undergraduates (REU) programs, an NSF International Research Experience for Students (IRES) International, and Beckman Scholars program. Staff FTE has fluctuated over the years to accommodate special projects and personnel availability.

VIGNETTE 3.3

Winny Dong, Director, Cal Poly Pomona Office of Undergraduate Research (OUR)

The Cal Poly Pomona Office of Undergraduate Research (CPP OUR) was established in August 2013 with a student success grant from the

Office of the Chancellor. (Cal Poly Pomona is part of the 23-campus California State University (CSU) system, overseen by the CSU Office of the Chancellor.) The original budget for the CPP OUR was $70,000 for the year, which included salaries, benefits, and anything else the office needed to function. Needless to say, we had to do a lot with very little. One of the best decisions we made was to put most of that money into hiring a half-time staff member. For the first two years, the OUR was made up of two part-time staff (a faculty director at 13% time and an associate at 50% time). Directing most of our funding toward the half-time associate meant that there was consistency in our activities and a reliable point of contact. The role of the faculty director was mostly to set the vision for the office and to build relationships across campus so that eventually we could garner more support from the university.

Another important role of the faculty director was (and continues to be) to seek external funding. During the first two years of establishing the OUR, we received a Title III grant from the US Department of Education and an S-STEM grant from the National Science Foundation. Funding from those two grants meant that we had high-profile programs that engaged students in research. Upper-level administrators were recruited to be on the advisory board for the grants and through those interactions we were able to show them the impact that undergraduate research had on student success, such as enhanced retention and graduation, and sense of belonging. This greatly increased the buy-in from the university and we now (as of Fall 2023) have a budget from the university that supports a full-time faculty director, full-time associate, student assistants, and funding to support student presentation at national conferences. We continue to rely on external funding for the bulk of student scholarships, research stipends, and programs that focus on specific student demographics.

The culture of engaging undergraduate students in research at Cal Poly Pomona was well established long before the creation of the OUR. When the OUR was first created, it was critical that we were very clear about the role of the OUR – we are here to support existing programs and not to replace them or to oversee their activities. The goals of the OUR are to support existing programs, to fill in any holes in student and faculty support, and to help existing programs work together and leverage their resources. One of the activities that won over the directors of pre-existing URSCA programs on campus was very simple – a joint calendar of workshops. This way the McNair director can see what LSAMP is offering and vice versa. This facilitated the sharing of common workshops such as GRE preparation, writing a personal statement, and overcoming the imposter phenomenon. Based on the feedback from existing URSCA programs, the OUR also began to organize events that served all URSCA programs such as annual student research conferences, multi-disciplinary summer research seminars, and faculty training on mentoring diverse students in research.

As the campus began to see the OUR as the clearinghouse of all things research, we began to offer more services that met the needs of the broader campus community. The OUR offered faculty members support in grant writing when they wanted to include undergraduate researchers in their grants. This resulted in the OUR being the Co-PI on several grants. We established the Faculty Mentor Stars program to recognize faculty mentors. We worked with the library to encourage students to publish their research results in the digital repository, Bronco ScholarWorks, and in return the library helps the OUR publish an annual student research journal called *Reach*. We coordinate the gathering of university-wide data on the percentage of students who participate in research and research-related activities (through an annual student survey) as well as graduate school attendance data (through the National Clearinghouse Database).

For additional information about the CPP OUR, we invite you to explore the following websites:

- CPP OUR, www.cpp.edu/our-cpp/index.shtml
- Recorded and current workshops, www.cpp.edu/our-cpp/events-workshops/workshops.shtml
- Faculty Mentor Stars, www.cpp.edu/our-cpp/mentors/stars/index.shtml
- For students, getting started in research resources, www.cpp.edu/our-cpp/students/getting-started.shtml
- Contact us page, www.cpp.edu/our-cpp/about/staff.shtml

Worksheet: staffing and tasks

Use this list to identify specific tasks your office will undertake. Next to each task you check, identify whom in your proposed office structure will do this work. Use the extra spaces at the end to include items specific to your mission.

Staffing and Tasks Checklist

Task   Person/role assigned to task

__ craft strategic plan
__ determine office budget
develop staffing plan
__ develop annual schedule or work plan
__ develop and manage advisory board
__ determine availability of on-campus research
   opportunities; develop new opportunities
__ connect students to on-campus opportunities
__ mentor relationships and communication
__ faculty/mentor support programs
__ connect students to summer / off-campus opportunities
__ academic and professional development workshops
__ undergraduate research courses
__ responsible conduct in research (RCR) training
__ support for student scholarship and fellowship applications
__ support for students attending conferences (academic)
__ on campus research events
__ marketing and outreach
__ communications (email blasts, flyers, newsletters, website,
   research journal, etc.)
__ fundraising and grant writing
__ grant programs for students and/or mentors
__ data collection
__ program assessment
__ annual or final reporting
__ end of year or other celebratory events recognizing students
   and mentors
__ communicate accomplishments to campus administration
__ general office functions
__ manage office budget
__ process student or mentor payments
__ support for students attending conferences (administrative);
   process student travel
__ organize meetings (advisory board, etc.)
__ oversee process for academic credit
__ develop and oversee peer to peer programs
__ develop campus partnerships
__ community-based research
__ international opportunities
__ connecting to the national conversation: CUR, NCUR,
   SACNAS, other disciplinary organizations connected
   to URSCA
__ (add your own here)

Figure 3.2 Staffing and tasks checklist.

Notes

1 More information can be found at mentorcollective.org. This mention is in no way an endorsement of a particular program or platform, as we have not utilized these in our own work. Often companies offering such services will attend the Council on Undergraduate Research (CUR) annual conferences. Speaking to company representatives, as well as your colleagues who utilize their services is the best way to determine the best fit for your campus or program.
2 Undergraduateresearch.princeton.edu/programs/rematch
3 See lsa.umich.edu/urop.research-mentors.html or csumb.edu/uroc/become-uroc-mentor/
4 Kinkead, Joyce and Linda Blockus. *Undergraduate Research Offices and Programs: Models and Practices.* The Council on Undergraduate Research, 2012.
5 The document, as well as additional tools, is available here: www.cur.org/engage/mentors/coeur/
6 The broad outline of considerations is as follows, but the document digs deeply into each of these to describe the ideal areas of commitment and support that a campus should consider: (I) campus mission and culture; (II) administrative support; (III) [campus] research infrastructure; (IV) [faculty] professional development opportunities; (V) [faculty] recognition; (VI) dissemination; (VII) student-centered issues; (VIII) curriculum; (IX) summer research program; (X) assessment; (XI) strategic planning.
7 In 2020, the conference was canceled due to the COVID-19 pandemic.

References

Characteristics of Excellence in Undergraduate Research. Edited by Nancy Hensel, 2012, www.cur.org/assets/1/23/COEUR_final.pdf
Kinkead, J., and L. Blockus, editors. *Undergraduate Research Offices & Programs: Models & Practices.* Council on Undergraduate Research, 2012, pp. 95–122.

4 Ready, set, go! Goals for the first year

As with many academic initiatives, deliberate planning and implementation in the first year is especially critical for establishing long-term success. Once you have put your academic, staffing, and logistical plans in place along the lines suggested in Chapters 2 and 3, it's time to get down to the nitty-gritty: what to do during the first academic year cycle of your new undergraduate research, scholarship, and creative activity (URSCA) center? We outline here a timeline and areas that we think are especially important to focus on during the exciting first year. We are structuring the timeline based on the start of the academic year, as that is when many centers first dig into their work – but it could be modified of course depending on when your center begins operations.

First term (fall semester or quarter):

1. Getting the word out – advertising and recruitment
2. Student URSCA participation selection
3. Planning for continued/sustainable funding
4. Planning for end-of-year student showcase

Second term (winter and spring quarters/spring semester):

5. Research/creative activity placements
6. Begin student participant data collection
7. Continued recruitment

Third term (summer):

8. URSCA activities
9. Dissemination (summer's end symposium)
10. Secure/procure continued funding

DOI: 10.4324/9781003154952-4

We'll examine each of these in more detail. Again, these are suggestions regarding where your effort will likely most be needed; as circumstances vary, some may be more important than others for your nascent center.

First term

Getting the word out – advertising and recruitment

You'll want to start advertising for student participants and research/ scholarly mentors as soon as you get confirmation that your nascent center is a go. The first autumn term is a time to meet with students (preferably in orientation sessions, and/or in classes early in the term) and faculty to let them know about your wonderful new opportunities. While you'll inevitably start with a small-ish cohort your first year, it's important to target your messaging to the students you want to serve, both in terms of majors and in terms of demographics. Including lower-division students by advertising in first-year seminar courses is always a good idea, as you may need several rounds of advertising over the years to fully recruit the breadth and volume of students you want to eventually serve.

Student URSCA participation selection

Starting out, you may be inclined to be less selective in choosing your first cohort of student participants. However, you'll want to be sure that you've got some sort of meaningful application process in place. This serves two purposes. First, you'll need a way to ensure that prospective students are eligible for the funding support that you have procured – in some cases, you'll be restricted by demographics or major, etc. Second, you'll want to establish standards for participation, calibrated to the type of program you're building. Does your center aim to get students into the most competitive Ph.D. programs? Are you looking to expand access to high-impact practices? You can calibrate your application process to reflect the nature of your program, and, once you have it in place, you'll be able to rely on it to vet potential participants as your program grows. Creating an evaluation committee comprised of staff, faculty, and administrators who are committed to the development of your center is a great way to start things off, even with a potentially small number of applicants in the first year.

Planning for continued/sustainable funding

From the get-go, you'll need to be concerned with continuity and sustainability of your program. Although it's nice to get seed money from your campus or elsewhere to start an undergraduate research initiative, it will be imperative to form a plan from the beginning to continue your center's activities – as they say, it's a marathon, not a sprint. Think about the next 5–10 years, and where funding will come from as your center gains momentum. It's also useful to think about what your center might look like without you or any of the current staff involved – including supportive administrators. How will things continue to serve students after you are gone? It may seem premature to think about things like succession planning, but many well-intended initiatives begin with a promising future and fizzle after a year or two because, once the excitement dies down, there is no long-term plan for sustainability. That plan should include frank discussions with campus partners about institutionalizing some or all of the elements essential to your center, from staffing to ongoing operational costs.

Planning for end-of-year student showcase and/or celebration

An important element of your program is providing a space/place/time for your URSCA students to showcase their work. This will require coordinating a whole suite of logistics, including securing a venue, arranging for catering, and potentially recruiting poster and talk judges. Because space and time around the end of the academic year are often full with a host of activities (e.g., capstone presentations, affinity group celebrations, and commencement activities), we recommend starting the process as early as possible. You may want to combine an end-of-year URSCA showcase with a special graduation send-off for your students, or you may want the latter to be a separate, more intimate event with student families and friends. We have found a small, casual year-end celebration for our scholars is also a great place to honor and showcase research mentors (including a mentor-of-the-year presentation), which requires further advance planning and coordination. Taken together, it's not too early to design and start to plan logistics in the first term of the year.

Second term

Research/creative activity placements

During the early part of the second term (e.g., after winter break) is a good time to start getting students matched up with URSCA placements for the upcoming summer. This is especially important if your office will assist students in finding external opportunities – many organized summer research programs and Research Experience for Undergraduates (REUs) are moving application deadlines back to the December–February period. Be sure to familiarize yourself with current deadlines and plan ahead. An effective way to start this is to give students some training and agency in procuring their own placements/funds; we normally have a training camp, for instance, that emphasizes the importance of procuring funding – along with specific suggestions/tips – for students coming into our programs. Placements can sometimes take several months to lock down – especially if any brokering in terms of fiscal/logistical support needs to be done (e.g., an REU program at a different university may invite one of your students to participate but only if they can provide their own travel expenses or housing), so it's best to hit the ground running.

Begin student participant data collection

Halfway through the first academic year is a good time to start collecting student data in earnest. This will include all manner of data, including the usual demographic information along with more specialized characteristics, for example, major, previous URSCA experiences, etc. Most important will be to organize and prepare for data collection – and because you hope to continue a robust assessment of your program for years to come, you'll want to ensure you have a sound protocol in place that is supported by other units on campus as well (including your institutional assessment office/team). We find it's always better to lay the groundwork for important data collection efforts well ahead of time, so there are no surprises – and no lost data or time wasted chasing information after the fact. Chapter 11 in this volume will provide a more detailed look into assessment and educational research.

Continued recruitment

As is often the case with educational interventions, it seems as though you've barely begun when you need to start planning/implementing your next year's activities. It's important to think about recruiting strategies for your next round/cohort of student participants. At this time, you might consider a mid-year recruitment for filling any slots/capacity you have in the current cohort of students; likewise, you'll want to start thinking about putting protocols in place for recruiting students who may want to conduct/continue research after the summer.

Third term (summer)

URSCA activities

This will be the focus of the program for your students – placements finalized, preparations complete, and students will be excited to engage in their various URSCA activities. While your staff will be rightfully relieved to have gotten all preparations done and to have the actual research/scholarly activities underway, you'll want to be ready to problem solve as issues come up – especially for remote URSCA projects. Even though you will have tried to address common issues that might arise with your students engaging in new and challenging activities, potentially in a new and challenging environment, you'll invariably have to deal at some point with unforeseen events. It's good to have your team on hand to address, in a timely manner, any issues that might arise, ranging from last-minute housing glitches to homesickness to any miscommunications that may arise between students and their research mentors/partners. All of which is to say that summer can be a relatively easy and uneventful time in the center's lifecycle – but be prepared to meet glitches as they arise!

Dissemination (summer's end symposium)

The end of the summer URSCA activities is an exciting time – and a great opportunity to hold a symposium in which students can show off their projects and disseminate their results. This is often one of the most enjoyable occasions for URSCA center staff – one in which students return brimming with confidence and new-found scholarly identity, eager to showcase their achievements in front of family, friends, and colleagues. We find that holding such an event close to the beginning of the fall term can make it more feasible that parents and faculty (who may be off-contract in summer) attend. However, scheduling it too close to the start of the fall term can mean overlap with orientation events and meetings, running the risk of having your event eclipsed by myriad other campus events tightly scheduled before the start of term. It's worth putting some thought into how you'll want to navigate these tradeoffs; on our campus [California State University, Monterey Bay (CSUMB)], we have found that it's better to hold the symposium several weeks before the start of term, simply from a logistical point of view, despite the tradeoffs.

Secure/procure continued funding

Even before the dust settles on your summer-end event, you'll want to be thinking about procuring continued funding for your center activities. Ideally, you will have something lined up before the end of your first year, as you'll need ample lead time for planning, and recruiting students and faculty mentors – and you'll want to take advantage of the momentum of a successful first year. Internal funding will likely be the easiest and simplest

way to ensure continued activities, but you'll want to also consider supporting any bridge/temporary funding your campus has allocated to you
with external funding for sustainability (see the above note on sustainability, and Chapter 8 for more on funding). At this point in the cycle, you
should have things wrapped up or close to being wrapped up – and possibly use positive outcomes on display in your campus summer-end event
to provide compelling evidence of funding deservedness.

While we close this chapter with a sample year-long planning guide or
workplan, these are, in our estimation, the bare minimum elements of
planning and implementation that you'll need to consider for a successful
first year. There may be other considerations particular to your situation –
including challenges associated with administrative structure, funding,
and other idiosyncrasies related to your campus – but these should provide
you with a good start.

This timeline, developed by Bobby Quiñonez of CSUMB's Undergraduate Research Opportunities Center (UROC) program, represents the
annual activities for a more established URSCA operation and can serve as
a template as you plan your first year, then expand, and revise your activities
as your program grows.

UROC ANNUAL TIMELINE (sample)

Fall

- RSCH 300 and 400 courses offered.
- Work with individual students on graduate school and fellowship applications, and, as needed, assist faculty with letters of support.
- Administer post-research surveys to students and follow-up surveys to alumni to gain feedback on the research experience and the mentoring received.
- Recruit UROC students, including a new cohort of McNair Scholars.
- Order UROC Portfolios (if needed)
- Convene the fall meeting of the UROC advisory board.
- Host UROC fall workshops: Graduate School Applications, Statements of Purpose, and Applying for Research Experiences for Undergraduates (REU) programs.
- Fall student-based conferences: the national conference of the Society for the Advancement of Chicanos and Native Americans in Science (SACNAS); and the Annual Biomedical Research Conference for Minority Students (ABRCMS).
- Conduct orientation events for students transferring from community colleges.
- Start Goldwater Scholarship process (due January; timeline outlined below).
- Start Udall Scholarship process (due early March).

Figure 4.1 Sample UROC annual timeline.

Winter

- Annual Performance Reports for McNair and HSI STEM & Articulation.
- Revise the curriculum for the fall research seminar course.
- Prepare for spring research seminar courses.
- Identify UR grant opportunities and begin proposal writing.
- Draft UROC's annual report.
- Recruit and help students prepare for the CSU system's annual research competition.
- Work with faculty on inquiry-based, applied-learning curricula and assessment tools.
- Pull Fall grades and send Academic Warning Letters as needed.
- Prepare
- Winter Newsletter.
- Verify number of Stoles needed for Graduation.
- Start CSUPERB Presidents' Commission Scholars Program Applications (due mid February).

Spring

- RSCH 200 and 301 courses offered.
- CSU Student Research Competition.
- Pre-Doctoral Scholars Applications Due.
- Host UROC spring workshops: Graduate School 101, Graduate Record Examination Training, Career Panels, and Preparing for the Summer Research Experience.
- Conduct annual Mentor Training Workshop.
- Convene Spring UROC advisory committee meeting.
- Celebrate National Undergraduate Research Week.
- Spring student-based conferences: Northern California Forum for Diversity in Graduate Education and National Conference on Undergraduate Research (NCUR).
- Place UROC students in summer research opportunities (identify opportunities, negotiate placements, and place students).
- Work with students to develop their research planning guides.
- Conduct pre-research experience survey and focus groups.
- Prepare speakers for Year End Celebration.
- Host year-end UR events.
- Produce the annual summary of our students' summer research placements and a description of where our UROC seniors will be attending graduate school.
- Identify UROC Mentor Award Recipient.
- Update placements (May).

Summer

- Revise curricula for research seminar courses.
- Pull Fall grades and send Academic Warning Letters as needed.
- UROC staff present program and research results at CUR and other conferences.
- Conduct mid-summer check-ins with all UROC students and mentors and review students' reflective writing about their summer research experiences.
- Conduct orientation events for students transferring from community colleges.
- Produce UROC's strategic plan for the coming year.
- Update UROC Fast Facts.
- Produce materials for advisory committee.
- Summer Newsletter.

Figure 4.1 (Continued)

Ongoing

- Place UROC students in research positions, and develop or revise learning outcomes as needed
- Conduct review sessions to prepare students for research presentations.
- Work with faculty on inquiry-based, applied-learning curricula and assessment tools.
- Conduct private fundraising activities.
- Identify UR grant opportunities and write proposals.
- Produce new marketing materials and videos.
- Revise and improve UROC website.
- Expand research opportunities for UROC students at public and private organizations.

Figure 4.1 (Continued)

5 Finding funding to support students, mentors, and your programmatic needs

No matter how much passion and excitement the prospect of creating an undergraduate research center generates, you will eventually need to move beyond personal/institutional capital and find funding to support all of the elements required to run a smooth operation. Ideally, you'll garner financial support from a diverse portfolio of sources ranging from federal grants, to foundation support and private donors. Furthermore, you may be able to procure funds from your campus or campus system if appropriate. This chapter will provide strategies and resources for finding funding to support URSCA.

Individually mentored research/scholarly activities, traditionally the norm for STEM fields, are the most expensive type of undergraduate research to fund – and the focus of most nascent undergraduate research programs. Increasingly, however, campuses looking to align curricular and co-curricular activities – as well as broaden access to undergraduate research experiences – are revising curricula to include more Course-based Undergraduate Research Experiences (CUREs). This approach can coincide with departmental/college unit curriculum reviews – and can also afford economies of scale to support research for large numbers of students.

With respect to individually mentored research activities, our philosophy is that students should receive some form of compensation when conducting research that is above and beyond what they would normally do in courses, labs, senior capstone projects, or other university degree requirements. This is really a practical as well as a philosophical stance: funding undergrads engaged in co-curricular research activities serves not only as an incentive but also as a strategic means of clearing away distractions (obviating the need to work long hours at an unrelated job, etc.) so that they can really focus on their scholarly work. Because of this, a large focus of our administrative attention (as well as student learning) is on finding and procuring research funding.

As you develop your funding strategies, keep in mind that funding availability – the types and amounts – can play an important role in addressing equity issues on your campus. Because this may not be immediately obvious to everyone, it can be important (practically,

DOI: 10.4324/9781003154952-5

philosophically, ethically, and pedagogically) to couch your funding needs in terms of diversity and inclusion. Underrepresented students – including first in family to go to college, low income, and transfer students, in addition to students from groups traditionally underrepresented in higher education – benefit disproportionately more than other students from engagement in high-impact practices (HIPs) such as undergraduate research.[1] At the same time, these types of students often have more difficulties finding their way into participating in undergraduate research.[2] This makes providing funding for students from widely diverse backgrounds absolutely essential – and it can go a long way toward creating a more inclusive campus culture.[3]

Federal funding

Happily, federal funding for undergraduate research has expanded dramatically over the past ten years. The National Science Foundation, US Department of Education, US Department of Agriculture, and National Institutes of Health all have grant programs that explicitly aim to bolster efforts to engage undergraduates in faculty-mentored research in the sciences. Furthermore, they increasingly are earmarking funds to support initiatives at Hispanic-Serving Institutions (HSIs) or Minority-Serving Institutions (MSIs). The National Science Foundation has long-standing alliance programs such as the Louis Stokes Alliance for Minority Participation that increasingly supports undergraduate research activities in STEM fields, and the US Department of Education McNair Scholars Program allows for heavy investment in student participation across all disciplines in scholarly/research activities as a major component of preparing underserved student populations for graduate school. Finally, many campuses are able to leverage other funding housed in student success programs (e.g., TRIO) to create and sustain undergraduate research experiences; work-study funding may also be a good source of undergraduate research support for eligible students.

Strategically, we like to think about leveraging federal funding support across initiatives in order to maximize effectiveness and student servingness. For instance, at one of our institutions (CSU Monterey Bay), the campus was able to procure an HSI-STEM and Articulation grant from the US Department of Education to support undergraduate research engagement. The capacity-building nature of this type of grant also allowed for boosting faculty resources; faculty were able to use the grant to build up their research labs with much-needed lab equipment/supplies and also benefit from a faculty fellows training program in developing CUREs that our grant supported. These resources then facilitated further undergraduate research participation, both in individually mentored research experiences as well as through curricular changes and more CUREs. Furthermore, the increase in interest in CUREs led to more departments on campus finding more funding to support more faculty development and curricular change. Leveraging funds in this way can boost the chances of procuring funding as well as increase the likelihood that your campus will institutionalize the practices you establish in your grant-funded initiatives.

In a more focused way, our campus also procured funding from the US Department of Agriculture aimed at increasing Latinx student participation in agricultural and food sciences, in collaboration with a local R1 institution with great expertise in these disciplines (University of California, Santa Cruz). This funding helped establish a pipeline between our campuses that increased student and faculty/staff interactions as well as both undergraduate and graduate research and teaching opportunities between the two schools. The funding, along with targeted hiring and curricular revisions in the College of Science on our campus, has led to a spate of more resources, including five-year USDA NEXTGEN grants awarded to both campuses to bolster both curricular and URSCA student opportunities and success.

Federal Funding Opportunities to support Undergraduate Research

US Department of Education

- *Hispanic-Serving Institution STEM and Articulation Grants.* Large capacity-building grants aimed at (1) increasing the number of Hispanic and other low-income students attaining degrees in the fields of science, technology, engineering, or mathematics; and (2) developing model transfer and articulation agreements between two-year and four-year institutions in STEM fields.
- *Ronald E. McNair Post-Baccalaureate Achievement Program.* Supports opportunities for research or other scholarly activities; summer internships; seminars and other educational activities designed to prepare students for doctoral study; tutoring; academic counseling; and activities designed to assist students participating in the project in securing admission to and financial assistance for enrollment in graduate programs. *Supports both STEM and non-STEM student activities.*

National Science Foundation

- *Improving Undergraduate STEM Education (IUSE).* Supports projects to improve STEM teaching and learning for undergraduate students. Special *RFP for HSIs:* Supports projects that improve undergraduate STEM education and increase the rates of recruitment, retention, and graduation of undergraduate STEM students at Hispanic-Serving Institutions.
- *Louis Stokes Alliance for Minority Participation (LSAMP).* Supports university alliances and post-baccalaureate fellowship programs focused on increasing the number of STEM bachelor's and graduate degrees awarded to populations historically underrepresented in STEM fields.
- *Research Experiences for Undergraduates (REU).* Supports active research participation by undergraduate students in any of the areas of research funded by the National Science Foundation.

National Institutes of Health

- *Genome Research Experiences to Attract Talented (GREAT) Undergraduates into the Genomics Field to Enhance Diversity.* Supports collaborative institutional partnerships that provide research education programs for undergraduates enrolled at Minority-Serving Institutions (MSIs) or Institutional Development Award (IDeA)-eligible institutions. A partnership will include an MSI or IDeA-eligible institution, and one or more research-intensive institutions or organizations with a suitable research base for graduate-level training in scientific areas of interest to the National Human Genome Research Institute (NHGRI).

US Department of Agriculture

- *Agriculture and Food Research Initiative – Education and Workforce Development (EWD).* Focuses on developing the next generation of research, education, and extension professionals in the food and agricultural sciences.
- *Hispanic-Serving Institutions Education Grants Program.* Promotes and strengthens the ability of HSIs to carry out higher education programs to attract, retain, and graduate outstanding students capable of enhancing the nation's food, agriculture, natural resources, and human sciences professional and scientific workforce.

Non-federal funding sources: foundations and individual donors

On the private donor front, it's important to work closely with your advancement/development office. First steps include cultivating a relationship with – ideally – a dedicated development and/or foundation relations officer. Campus development staff can help you generate modest but important start-up funds through, for example, simple crowd-sourcing campaigns, and can help advise on your inclusion in annual campus giving days/fund drives. Through more extensive discussions with development staff, you can outline the vision, mission, and anticipated activities that your center will develop; this will help when pitching more substantive funding requests to private or Foundation donors. This may involve having your team tailor messages about your center to appeal to potential donors, calling out specifics (e.g., involvement of underrepresented students in certain disciplines such as women in STEM) that might be especially alluring and meaningful for community donors. You may also develop a one-pager with your development office that distills your goals and funding needs into an easy reference sheet suitable for presentation and dissemination to potential donors.

In addition to partnering with your development office, you'll want to think about linking student success with opportunities in the local workforce; examples abound of creative university partnerships with local industry. Loyola Marymount University leveraged new mechanical engineering laboratory facilities to partner with a local manufacturing firm as undergraduates engaged in the process of testing sensors that the company wanted to deploy in local weirs and flumes to measure water flow. Students worked under the guidance of a faculty member and also adhered to strict company protocols, learning both techniques and business aspects in a rigorous and authentic way. This eventually led to further opportunities for faculty and students through the development of contracts that support research activities as well as product development, a win–win for the university and its regional industry partners.[4]

Private foundations may be the best source of funding for student opportunities outside the STEM fields, as they have particular areas of focus that often align with academic work being done across the humanities and arts. Foundations can be a source of seed funding for your research center that may be leveraged with other sources of support for the arts and humanities. At UC Merced, for instance, funding from the Mellon Foundation has allowed the campus to build a robust *Undergraduate Research in the Humanities* ("UROC-H") program. Providing funding for both faculty and undergraduates who work together on humanities research, the program focuses on research clusters, in which students sign up to work as part of a team on faculty-mentored projects.[5]

While foundations can be an excellent funding source, it's worth noting that they often are interested in investing in programs that support their funding interests or initiatives. As such, you'll want to be sure to work with your development/foundation relations team to craft an application that focuses on academic or student success goals as related to those funding interests. Furthermore, it will be important to indicate your plans for how your campus initiatives will continue with additional/alternative support once the foundation support is complete. Examples of foundations that have funded URSCA centers and programs include the Mellon Foundation, the Research Corporation for Scientific Advancement, the Chan Zuckerberg Initiative, the Koret Foundation, the Howard Hughes Medical Institute, and others.

VIGNETTE 5.1

Jenny Olin Shanahan, Bridgewater State University

Alumni and foundation support

URSCA offers a compelling draw for alumni and foundation support, especially because student success in URSCA represents the best of an institution's commitment to inclusive excellence. At Bridgewater State University (BSU) in Massachusetts, the university foundation dedicated $50,000 to found the URSCA program in 1999. Since then, gifts from alumni and friends of the institution have helped support URSCA in two principal ways: (a) endowed funds sponsored by particular graduating classes and (b) current-use funds designated in annual giving campaigns.

At milestone reunions (e.g., as we plan for the Class of 2000's 25th anniversary in 2025), colleges and universities often ask alumni of that graduating class for a special gift dedicated to a selected institutional need. BSU's Office of Alumni Affairs has asked for several class gifts for URSCA conference travel grants.

At institutions like ours, with a majority of students from underserved groups, including BIPOC, low-income, and first-generation students, expecting undergraduates to fund even a portion of travel, lodging, meals, and registration fees for conferences is not often tenable. Graduates of the institution know that reality well, from their own and/or their classmates' experiences. We have found that alumni donors need no convincing about the transformative power of travel, as well as of networking, learning, and presenting at conferences in one's chosen field, which has made focusing our alumni requests on URSCA travel grants a perfect choice.

Alumni often give higher-than-usual amounts on distinctive occasions such as milestone reunions. Their special class gifts can be pooled and invested as an endowed fund, and the interest generated by the investment transferred annually into the specified operating budget. In the BSU example, endowed class gifts defray the costs of undergraduate conference travel. As a result of four graduating classes' selection of URSCA conference travel for their reunion gifts (including the Class of 1952s large 50th reunion gift in 2002), BSU sends dozens of students to national and regional conferences every year, all expenses paid, to present their research/scholarship. At homecoming, some of the students who benefited from those endowed funds are invited to share their work with the alumni in attendance.

BSU's development staff also lists URSCA as one of the options to which donors can designate their gifts on the university's annual Giving Day, through mail-in envelopes placed within the alumni magazine, and via the "donate" button on the website. Those designated funds are transferred to the URSCA operating budget each fiscal year. We apply those "current use" funds to everything from our annual symposia to students' summer research stipends.

The key to inspiring philanthropic gifts to URSCA, whether by alumni classes or individual donors, is telling compelling stories about URSCA in multiple places over time. At BSU, those of us involved in URSCA collaborate with colleagues in enrollment, marketing, and communications as well as outreach and engagement (the division that includes development and alumni affairs) to identify promising topics and help explain the significance of URSCA. Those topics include student and mentor profiles and news about undergraduate researchers' and artists' publications, awards, and other achievements. The stories range from news briefs to in-depth magazine articles and appear in the university's social media, websites, print magazines, newsletters, brochures, and admissions' materials.

The prevalence and diversity of URSCA stories convey the value the institution places on that high-impact practice. Then, when alumni and friends see requests for URSCA support, they know something about the program and how it benefits students. University news stories don't typically include appeals for funding, and they don't need to. They set the stage for donations over time, simultaneously inspiring financial support and offering evidence that URSCA-designated gifts make tangible differences in the lives of students.

Campus partners

The Sponsored Programs office is a key ally you'll want to cultivate when planning for federal support for your program. Staff responsible for pre- and post-award logistics can be a tremendous help in tracking grant deadlines, regulations, and general trajectory of funding as you build your portfolio. They can also alert you to appropriate/new funding opportunities as they learn of them through their networks. If your campus has a Research Development office, you will want to work closely with them in these efforts.

As mentioned in Chapter 2, it's essential to develop strong campus partnerships in order to build a diverse and comprehensive support system. One of the most important connections you'll want to cultivate is with the financial aid office. While it's ideal to provide funding for undergraduates engaged in research/scholarly activities as salary/wages, state and federal restrictions may restrict you to providing funding via financial aid disbursements. This is not as ideal for a not-so-obvious yet common reason: if students have any outstanding tuition or other fees in their accounts, your research disbursement will go immediately toward paying that off, preventing the student from having access to that money when they are actually conducting their research (hence, removing one of the immediate advantages of paid research work). In other cases, your research support funding may collide with other scholarships awarded to students – with restrictions about how much the students can accept. A critical element in these circumstances is to communicate early and often with your financial aid office – they can help you understand the timing of financial aid disbursement and hopefully suggest ways of working with your students to minimize any such surprises/unintended consequences. If you are in a state-system, there may be collective initiatives/solutions to these types of challenges; in California, legislation is in the works aimed at unblocking student access to overlapping funding so that they aren't left struggling to make ends meet while conducting URSCA activities simply because they accepted state aid earlier in the year.

As you work to garner private/foundation and state/federal funding, it's worth checking out smaller campus funds that are earmarked for student success endeavors that could include undergraduate research. Coordinating with faculty applying for small development grants related to research, coupled with any travel funding available on campus for faculty and students, may be a first step to getting undergrads involved in research, even if it's only to attend/present at a conference with their mentor. Student fee programs on campus can also be a source of support for URSCA activities. These are small fees collected from each student upon registration that are then applied to a variety of programs across campus. Some campuses have open calls for proposals to secure funds to support student success – including engagement in high-impact practices. Although they generally offer smaller amounts, consider going after these types of funds to support important URSCA elements such as student travel to present results at regional or national conferences – something that may not be covered in other student success programs. Internal campus fee requests are generally not too complicated and can generate funding that aligns nicely with larger campus needs, thus multiplying the number of students your center can serve. At some institutions, the student senate has voted to earmark some of their funds, often generated by student fees, to support URSCA activities such as travel. And many universities have long-standing traditions of funding all students who get accepted to NCUR, WorldCUR, or similar conferences. This might be a tradition worth initiating.

Doing more with less

Starting off, undergraduate research centers (like most co-curricular offices that don't necessarily have dedicated central campus budget allocations) may consist of a single director (often a faculty member supported by a course buyout or some modest summer salary) and a half- or full-time administrative coordinator. In these beginning stages of development, it's critical to demonstrate "proof of concept"; rather than worry about expanding access, the early stage is a time for establishing procedures, developing best practices, and building infrastructure that will deliver solid scaffolding for your research students and their mentors. This seemingly Herculean task should be performed with an eye toward phase two, in which your campus is wowed by the impressive outcomes you and your students have been able to achieve – with the promise of sustainability, increased equity and access, and consistent quality that can be scaled up with more campus support. Discussions along these lines cannot start too early – your campus administrators should know that you'll be seeking further support for the initiative they have asked you to develop. Regular meetings along with transparent conversations about where and when you'll move to the next level of campus support/buy-in are critical.

In the current era of fiscal uncertainty in higher education, it's important to acknowledge that your center may have lean times, even right from the start, with which you'll have to contend. As colleges struggle with declining enrollments and demographic cliffs, adjusting to the boom and bust cycle of funding may require some creative problem-solving; in our experience, it's best to follow that old adage and plan for the best but prepare for the worst. One way to do this is to create multiple undergraduate programs, some of which (following best practices) offer students stipends and ample financial support for research experiences, others of which offer, say, academic credit but no financial support for research activities. At California State University, Monterey Bay (CSUMB), we offer a range of programs with overlapping curricula and goals so that we can provide opportunities for a wider range of students (see the text box, below).

Example: UROC programs at CSUMB offer both financial support and course credit options for URSCA; options vary among the different programs

- *UROC and McNair Scholars program*: offers students paid research hours throughout the academic year and summer; prescribed two-year program with extensive scaffolding via seminars and workshops; application required. Has been funded by a variety of federal grants, including from the Department of Education, the National Science Foundation, the National Institutes of Health, and the US Department of Agriculture.
- *UROC Researchers*: offer students paid *or* for-credit research options to engage in single-term faculty-mentored URSCA, with some scaffolding via workshops and individual advising.
- *Research Rookies*: self-guided online introduction to research consisting of nine mandatory activities and several optional ones. Aimed at providing an entryway into URSCA for students with little or no experience. No compensation offered, but can be used as a gateway to more intensive programs and experiences.
- *Koret Scholars*: supports undergraduate student scholarly activities/research in the social sciences, along with scaffolding including writing support. Paid, with students eligible for stipends/scholarships along with research expenses.
- *LSAMP Scholars*: paid support for students to engage in STEM research – including international research opportunities. Part of a state-wide and nation-wide community of LSAMP programs funded by the National Science Foundation.
- *UROC workshop series*: free series of workshops open to all students across campus, including those who are doing independent study and individually mentored undergraduate research outside formal UROC programs. Offers professional development support ranging from CV writing to Graduate School 101.

Multiple levels of support can create continuity in your funding stream as well as provide multiple points of access for students on a variety of academic trajectories. Having a well-rounded portfolio can also hedge against temporal fluctuations in internal and external funding availability. We recommend developing these types of programs even in boom times and offering clear explanations to students and their faculty mentors of the full range of options available.

Personnel is another arena in which you may need to think creatively. If you're just starting out, it can be difficult to build more than a one- or two-person center. Leveraging the services your center will be providing toward other initiatives your campus is keen to implement may be a way to garner additional personnel support. For instance, if your internship center needs administrative support, perhaps you can argue for a shared position which might help with both internships, as well as help with research placements for your center. Discerning which way your Dean/Provost/President/Chancellor wants to grow programs and units on campus is an important strategic skill that you'll want to develop; this underscores the importance of growing your campus network as discussed earlier.

Community colleges

Community colleges are increasingly developing research experiences for their students in order to pave the pathway to four-year institutions and beyond.[6] One way of engaging community college students in URSCA is to partner with local four-year campuses that have undergraduate research opportunities in place already (see the Los Angeles Valley College vignette at the end of this chapter); there is increasing federal support from agencies such as NSF and USDA for developing these types of articulation pathways from two- to four-year colleges. Arguably the easiest way to introduce students at the community college level to authentic research activities is by incorporating them directly into course curricula (CUREs), though more campuses are developing infrastructure to support individually mentored research as well. The Community College Undergraduate Research Initiative (CCURI) is an excellent community college consortium program that integrates an inquiry-based teaching model into first-year classes, leading to further engagement in undergraduate research – they maintain a website that is an excellent and inspiring resource. As at four-year institutions, the impetus for developing CUREs may stem from the need for curriculum development/revision, which may allow for economies of scale. Chapter 11 has more in-depth discussions and examples of CURE programs, including regional collaborative efforts across campuses.

VIGNETTE 5.2   Harvey Mudd College

Yi-Chieh Wu, Katherine Van Heuvelen, and Nicole Wallens

Finding funding at a small liberal arts college (summer and academic year)

Founded in 1955, Harvey Mudd College (HMC) is a small liberal arts college of engineering, science, and mathematics with about 100 tenured or tenure-track faculty and about 900 students ("Mudders").[7] Research, scholarship, and experiential learning are integral to the college mission. Faculty are expected to engage in scholarship to stay current in their field and to bring current knowledge and best practices into the classroom, and all Mudders engage in experiential learning throughout the curriculum. The Core Curriculum, required of all students in their first four semesters, includes hands-on practicums in engineering and laboratories in the natural sciences. Additionally, during the academic year, many Mudders pursue independent study under the supervision of faculty, and every summer, roughly 200 students conduct research on campus through full-time paid positions. Since HMC is an undergraduate-only institution, students who engage in research with faculty are major contributors and commonly co-author manuscripts and present their work at conferences. A Mudder's undergraduate career culminates in a required capstone project during senior year, which takes the form of either an individual thesis project with faculty or a Clinic project, in which students work in teams of four or five to solve real-world, technical problems for non-profit or corporate sponsors. As a result of these undergraduate opportunities, close to 30% of graduates pursue postgraduate degrees in science and engineering, among the highest rates in the nation.[8]

HMC considers faculty to be teacher-scholars, and faculty are encouraged but not expected to apply for external funds. These funds provide the majority of financial support for scholarship at the college, and since 2017, 39 faculty have been awarded grants totaling more than $10 million. Most grants come from the National Science Foundation to support specific projects (RUI), early-career academics (CAREER, CRII, and LEAPS-MPS), programs (REU), or instrumentation (MRI). In addition, faculty have received support from other federal agencies, including the National Institutes of Health, the National Oceanic and Atmospheric Administration, and the Office of Naval Research, as well as from private foundations, including the Research Corporation for Scientific Advancement, the Howard Hughes Medical Institute, the Chan Zuckerberg Initiative, and the Mellon Foundation. Some faculty have joint grants with collaborators at other colleges or universities to support joint research or to support shared infrastructure. External grants differ in the amount of compensation provided to faculty who conduct summer scholarship and can range from no funding to a stipend equivalent to 2/9 of the faculty member's regular salary, depending on the program stipulations of the funding agency. The college provides a $500–1,000 incentive award for tenure-track and tenured faculty who raise outside funds for on-campus research, though these awards cannot be used for faculty stipends. Additionally, faculty are supported by the Office of Sponsored Research. Founded in May 2021, its mission is to foster a culture of scholarship and grant-seeking as integral to teaching, and to partner with faculty to develop strategies and access external resources for funding their research, scholarship, and creative work.

The college supports faculty and student scholarship through internal funds. New hires are offered a start-up package, which may include summer stipends for students and faculty; lab and computing equipment, supplies, and services; travel support for conferences and to visit collaborators; publication fees; and discretionary funds toward professional memberships and development. Additionally, every winter, faculty are invited to apply for HMC-sponsored faculty research grants. All full-time faculty (tenured, tenure-track, and visiting) and postdocs can submit short proposals, and awards are made in two categories. The first category supports summer research students who work on campus, and the awards include pay to support a student working full-time for ten weeks along with a small budget for supplies and travel. The second category supports faculty whose work does not involve undergraduates, and the awards can be used to support a range of scholarly and creative activities or a faculty stipend. The college-wide research committee, which includes a faculty member from each department and is headed by the Associate Dean of faculty, evaluates proposals on intellectual merit, potential impact on the faculty member's career, broader impact, and previous successes. The college also has targeted funds to support research in specific areas, for example, sustainability and the intersection of science and society, and to support student travel to conferences and scientific meetings. Additionally, many departments have funds to support student research, and some departments provide faculty with a small discretionary fund, the size of which varies by department. Some endowed professorships include funding for research, as well. Most internal research funds come through the Office of College Advancement, which works with both individual donors as well as external funders to support institutional initiatives through endowments and annual gifts and grants.

VIGNETTE 5.3   Creating undergraduate research opportunities
at a community college: partnerships for excellence

Dr. Becky Green-Marroquin and Pamela
Byrd-Williams (MSc), Los Angeles Valley College

In efforts to create undergraduate research opportunities for students at Los Angeles Valley College over the last 20 years, the faculty within the Biology Department have been instrumental in establishing partnerships with local universities. The support needed to establish and run research on our campus was non-existent. Our campus, which sits within the heart of California's San Fernando Valley and is a Hispanic-Serving Institution, prepares students for transfer with a majority of our students transferring to nearby California State University Northridge (CSUN) and UCLA with some to Cal State LA, USC as well as other UCs. Our close proximity to UCLA and CSUN has allowed for strong partnerships in this regard.

LAVC and UCLA

Los Angeles Valley College (LAVC) partnered with UCLA for a Summer Bridge Program for almost 20 years under two different grant directors. This program was intended to establish a bridge to UCLA with a few community colleges that eventually grew to six community colleges within the greater LA area and then back down to a few at the end of the program. Students from LAVC who had completed their Life Science series (General Bio 1, General Bio 2 along with a techniques class, the Science of Biotechnology) were invited to apply to the summer BRIDGE at UCLA where they participated in an undergraduate research project matched to their topic interest. The program targeted underrepresented students in STEM in efforts to increase diversity in STEM, particularly at UCLA. The students were paid a stipend while they attended the summer program and were provided a meal card for the campus. Community college faculty were paid an annual stipend to recruit students and to provide annual feedback to the program director as to the progress of the students who participated and report if they were applying to UCLA for transfer, or to another four-year institution.

Lessons learned

Recruiting efforts were generally never as large as expected. A majority of the students who applied felt they were on a pre-medical track and did not see the importance of research or how it applied to them.

Students who did apply did not always meet the academic standards of UCLA, and while community college faculty saw the potential of the students given the opportunity, appropriate guidance, and encouragement, their recommendations were not always fruitful.

Another issue of the program was the disparity of skillsets of the students. LAVC offered the techniques class (the science of biotechnology) which provided our students with lab skills that not all of the other campuses had available. This meant that the student applicants from the other community colleges were entering with a different skill set.

In speaking to some of the students who have moved on since then, the overall experience was helpful because they were provided exposure to the university experience before they transferred, as well as to the possibility of research and graduate school.

LAVC and CSUN

In partnership with CSUN, LAVC was one of four partners in the Promoting Opportunities for Diversity in Education and Research (BUILD PODER) Program. The goal of this program was to increase students' interest in biomedical research and nurture their interest in pursuing research careers, with a broader impact of enhancing the diversity of the STEM workforce through community and educational partnerships. Faculty and students participated in mentoring activities that focused on providing equity in education, and building research skills. Mentors and students furthered their knowledge by looking at their STEM journey through the lens of critical race theory over the one-year period with discussions on equity, inclusion, and diversity in STEM. For this program, students were recruited at their respective community colleges where they engaged in a research project with a community college faculty mentor during the academic year; during the summer students participated in programming at CSUN.

Research at the community college included students in both STEM and the social sciences, who completed literature reviews, and survey, field, or wet lab-related research. Students mentored at LAVC who participated in the wet lab experience learned tissue culture of mammalian cells, various microscopy techniques as well as DNA electrophoresis and SDS PAGE. Community college faculty also developed a Public Health for Social Justice Course that introduced health disparities research and the role of biomedical research in generating health equity.

Summer programming for the students at CSUN included summer internships, conference presentations, and a lab research skills class (Jumpstart). Students were provided a monthly stipend during the year at the community college, and also during their summer while at CSUN, along with a meal card. Students were also provided tutoring support while at their home campus. If the student transferred to CSUN and applied for the university program, they were provided 40–60% tuition assistance as well as a stipend and travel funds for any conferences attended.

Lessons learned

The hurdle of providing the wet lab experience at the community college campuses was exacerbated by the lack of grant/research infrastructure on our campus. Other difficulties included the timeline for ordering supplies, and the added work of balancing heavy teaching loads with time to mentor students performing research. Arranging travel for conferences was also new to the bureaucracy of a local campus within a district entity. By the third year of the program, we were able to shift the burden of paying the student stipends, travel funds, and ordering supplies to the CSUN campus, with the subaward to the community college campuses covering faculty mentor stipends.

Students who participated in this program found that the program was instrumental in helping them apply their academic skills to real-world settings, it helped them build networking and support systems among community college faculty as well as peers, and they developed collaboration skills and feelings of confidence as a scientist.

Notes

1 Jones, M.T., et al. "Importance of Undergraduate Research for Minority Persistence and Achievement in Biology." *Journal of Higher Education*, vol. 81 no. 1, 2010, 82–115, https://doi.org/10.1353/jhe.0.0082 and Kinzie, J., et al. "Promoting Persistence and Success of Underrepresented Students: Lessons for Teaching and Learning." *New Directions for Teaching and Learning*, vol. 2008 no. 115, 2010, 21–38. https://doi.org/10.1002/tl.323
2 National Academy of Sciences, et al. *Expanding Underrepresented Minority Participation: America's Science and Technology Talent at the Crossroads.* The National Academies Press, 2011, https://doi.org/10.17226/12984
3 Haeger, H., et al. "Creating More Inclusive Research Environments for Undergraduates." *Journal of the Scholarship of Teaching and Learning*, vol. 21 no. 1, 2021.

4 Ramirez, M., et al. "Creative Funding Strategies for Undergraduate Research at a Primarily Undergraduate Liberal Arts Institution." *CUR Quarterly*, vol. 36 no. 2, 2015, 5–8.
5 https://uroc.ucmerced.edu/uroc-h
6 Patton, M., and E. Hause. *Community College Undergraduate Research Experience Summit Proceedings Report.* American Association of Community Colleges, 2020, www.aacc.nche.edu/URESummit
7 Parts of this introduction are taken verbatim from pages on the Harvey Mudd College website, including www.hmc.edu/about-hmc/history/ and www.hmc.edu/admission/discover/academic/
8 Gordan et al. "NSF 22–321. Baccalaureate Origins of U.S. Research Doctorate Recipients." March 2022, https://ncses.nsf.gov/pubs/nsf22321

References

Gordan et al. "NSF 22-321. Baccalaureate Origins of U.S. Research Doctorate Recipients." March 2022, https://ncses.nsf.gov/pubs/nsf22321
Haeger, H., et al. "Creating More Inclusive Research Environments for Undergraduates." *Journal of the Scholarship of Teaching and Learning*, vol. 21 no. 1, 2021.
Jones, M.T., et al. "Importance of Undergraduate Research for Minority Persistence and Achievement in Biology." *Journal of Higher Education*, vol. 81 no. 1, 2010.
Kinzie, J., et al. "Promoting Persistence and Success of Underrepresented Students: Lessons for Teaching and Learning." *New Directions for Teaching and Learning*, vol. 2008 no. 115, 2008, 21–38, https://doi.org/10.1002/tl.323
National Academy of Sciences, et al. *Expanding Underrepresented Minority Participation: America's Science and Technology Talent at the Crossroads.* The National Academies Press, 2011.
Patton, M., and E. Hause. *Community College Undergraduate Research Experience Summit Proceedings Report.* American Association of Community Colleges, 2020, www.aacc.nche.edu/URESummit
Ramirez, M., et al. "Creative Funding Strategies for Undergraduate Research at a Primarily Undergraduate Liberal Arts Institution." *CUR Quarterly*, vol. 36 no. 2, 2015, 5–8.

6 Beyond the lab/studio/archive: professional development support for student researchers from across the disciplines

Introduction

Although there are not established norms for much of what is addressed in the first chapters of this book, there is general agreement on the types of educational and professional development assistance that can maximize students' undergraduate research experiences. This chapter will focus on what that support looks like, what makes it meaningful and impactful, and what learning outcomes are achieved.

We know that URSCA experiences have the power to engage students,[1] increase graduation rates,[2] and propel them to meaningful careers.[3] However, a negative experience can also lead students to believe that research is not for them. Sometimes these difficult experiences come from a mismatch between the mentor and the student. Chapter 7 will discuss faculty training that can minimize the mismatch. Negative research experiences can also arise because students do not know what to expect from a research experience, do not know how to communicate with their mentors, experience imposter phenomenon, or have not learned how to manage their time and stress appropriately. Even when students have a great research experience, they may need help with communicating their experience to their families and friends, summarizing their research for graduate programs or potential employers, understanding professional etiquette at conferences, presenting their research results, etc. Below are examples of professional development workshops that can facilitate a positive experience with research as well as help students get the most out of their research experience. The suggested workshops are divided into different parts of a student's research career.

Notes for all workshops

First and foremost, your undergraduate research office does not need to provide all of the workshops listed below. If your campus has established

DOI: 10.4324/9781003154952-6

research support programs, such as a National Science Foundation Louis Stokes Alliances for Minority Participation (NSF LSAMP) Program, a McNair Scholars Program, or other Bridge programs, they will likely already offer many of these workshops. The career center and student affairs division may also have similar workshops in some form. If your office is just getting off the ground, it is useful to conduct a survey of existing workshops and offer just one or two workshops for topics that are not already addressed. Do reach out to the other programs about cross-listing/marketing existing workshops and permission to send additional students to those workshops. Most often, the other student support and undergraduate research programs will appreciate reaching a broader audience for their existing workshops as well as having access to the additional material that you develop.

Second, although content is the most critical part of any workshop, the mode of delivery is important as well. For all the workshops below, consider who may be the best presenter to share the information. Do you think students would benefit from hearing about a particular topic from a specific speaker? For example, in sharing with students what it is like to enter a Ph.D. program, perhaps alumni from your program who are in their first or second year of graduate school would make a nice panel. Your career center can be a great resource to give a workshop about resumes and CVs. And a faculty member could be a wonderful resource on how to narrow the focus of a research project. Reaching out to alumni, your institution's career center, your student wellness team, faculty members at your institution who may have expertise in the topic, etc. will broaden the workshops' appeal as well as form the basis for potential future collaborations.

Third, students often internalize content if they are asked to teach others or reflect on their own experiences related to the topic. It may be useful, as part of any workshop, to ask students to write a note to their future self as a reminder of what they plan to do based on the workshop (there are multiple websites that can facilitate this activity, such as www.futureme.org/); ask students to form groups to discuss how their own experiences are reflected in the workshop's content; or ask participants to come up with a short manual to help future students learn about the workshop topic.

Workshops that support a student's research experience and process

The following workshops are commonly found in undergraduate research programs and offices. We will not go into depth about these workshops since they probably already exist on your campus in one form or another.

The list is meant as a reminder for what your office can look for when collaborating with other student support programs.

- *How to Get Started in Undergraduate Research*: this workshop is intended to introduce students to the benefits of research, whether they are considering attending graduate school or not. Share information with students about the programs that exist on and off campus. Include how to approach potential faculty mentors about joining a research project.
- *Narrowing the Focus of Your Research Project*: this workshop may benefit from having a panel of faculty mentors since the process can be quite different for different disciplines.
- *Conducting a Literature Review*: this workshop discusses the purpose of a literature review, how to read journal articles and texts effectively, and how to organize citations.
- *Effective Research Communication 1: Writing a Successful Abstract*: this workshop discusses the elements of a research abstract.
- *Effective Research Communication 2: Writing a Research Paper*: this workshop discusses the elements of a research paper. You can include the journal submission process in this workshop.
- *Effective Research Communication 3: Presentations*: this workshop discusses the differences between posters and oral presentations. Share with students the elements of a strong presentation in terms of visual aids, timing, audience engagement, etc. It is worthwhile to address the anxiety that many students feel about making presentations and strategies for managing that anxiety.

Professional development for the beginning researcher: suggested workshops

Workshop on effective mentor–mentee relationships for students

Because many students, especially traditionally under-served and first-generation college students, have not had significant experiences with positive mentoring, they often do not know how to approach potential mentors or what to expect from mentors. Suggested content includes:

- Introduction to mentoring and the concept that most successful people have multiple mentors throughout their life.
- Qualities to look for in potential mentors – based on professional goals, personal development goals, research interest, etc.
- Encouraging students to reflect on their own communication, learning, and work styles so that they can find a mentor that is a good match for them.

- Email template for how to approach potential mentors. Students often get stuck on this step because they don't know how to approach potential mentors. Providing them a template where they just have to plug in a few details about themselves can make a big difference in whether the students take that first step.
- Understanding mentor expectations and communicating one's own expectations. A sample of a mentor–mentee agreement can be helpful to normalize research expectations. At Cal Poly Pomona's OUR, we use this template developed by Dr. Trina McMahon at the University of Wisconsin, Madison: www.cpp.edu/our-cpp/documents/Mentoring_Toolkit/Contracts.pdf
- The importance of communicating the students' own academic, career, and mentoring expectations to their mentors.
- Probably the most important take-away from this workshop: most faculty members enjoy mentoring students and that joy comes from seeing students succeed and being part of the student's journey. Understanding this helps historically underserved students overcome the fear of "troubling" a faculty member with questions or requests for guidance.

Workshop on overcoming the imposter phenomenon

This is an important workshop because, although all students can at times experience feeling like an imposter, it has been shown that high-achieving underserved students are most likely to experience feeling this way.[4] This psychological phenomenon can significantly limit the academic and career aspirations of students who have not learned to identify and address these feelings. Suggested content for this workshop includes:

- The psychology behind the phenomenon. Understanding the science behind the imposter phenomenon can help students see this as part of the normal growth process, and not as a weakness. This Ted talk by Elizabeth Cox provides a great introduction to imposter phenomenon and how you can combat it: www.ted.com/talks/elizabeth_cox_what_is_imposter_syndrome_and_how_can_you_combat_it
- The phenomenon is experienced by people across professions, educational level, and professional achievement. If the presenter has experiences in imposter phenomenon, it is helpful to share these personal experiences to help normalize these feelings.
- Ask students to reflect on situations when they have experienced feeling like an imposter and how they have dealt with the feeling in the past. If there are students who are willing to share their reflections, even better.

- Tools for overcoming the imposter phenomenon, such as recognizing triggers for the feeling, talking to others, and reflecting on and owning past successes. MindTools offers both an assessment and tools for overcoming imposter syndrome at: www.mindtools.com/azio7m7/impostor-syndrome
- It is important for students to internalize these ideas and tools. A good way to begin that process can be a group activity where students develop a toolkit to help others who experience the imposter phenomenon. Students are encouraged to be creative and the toolkits are shared publicly at the end of the workshop. In past workshops on our campus, student-developed toolkits have ranged from informational videos to a handout, a poem, a skit, and even a social media ad campaign.

Workshop on team-building and effective communication

Helping students learn how to communicate effectively and to value others who may not think like them is a critical part of the research process. Although this workshop is not focused on cultural diversity, students have reported using these skills to navigate culturally diverse teams and spaces.

- The workshop can start with students' self-assessment of strengths and workstyles via the Clifton Strength Quest, or a similar workstyle/ strengths assessment. Information on the Cliften Strength Quest can be found here: www.rand.org/education-and-labor/projects/assessments/ tool/1999/clifton-strengthsfinder.html. This helps students better understand their own strengths along with how their strengths have helped them succeed and how to best utilize these strengths for future success.
- Asking students to share their strengths and how they affect the students' workstyles will open the door for students to discuss how people with different strengths (and weaknesses) can work together effectively. This can be accomplished by the following exercise.
  - Students are first grouped with others with similar strengths to discuss their preferred working conditions and how they relate to others. This is shared with all groups at the end of the discussion period.
  - Students are then grouped with participants with different strengths to discuss what it is like to work with people with a variety of strengths and how the group can best communicate and work effectively with each other. This is also shared with all groups.
- It is useful to anchor the student group discussions with an understanding of the characteristics of constructive and destructive communication styles. A useful tool for describing these to students can be found at: https://matterapp.com/blog/the-primary-difference-between-constructive-feedback-and-destructive-feedback-is

Professional development for the more experienced researcher: suggested workshops

Workshop on professional etiquette: conferences, interviews, and other professional interactions

It is important to introduce students, especially first-generation college students, to the norms and expectations in different types of professional interactions they may encounter in college, the workplace, and graduate school. Understanding these norms and how to meet expectations helps students develop confidence and a stronger sense of belonging in higher education as well as in their future careers. Discussion topics can include:

- Professional attire for meetings, conferences, and interviews. It is important to acknowledge that the norm for this can differ quite a bit between different disciplines. Students should observe how faculty members dress, how invited speakers in their discipline dress, and ask their faculty mentors, graduate students, and postdocs about what is typically expected. However, general norms include ensuring that your ability and knowledge is not overshadowed by, for example, a particularly loud jacket – unless the jacket is part of what you would like to express to those you are meeting.
- How to make small talk at conferences and other networking opportunities.
- Students also learn how to prepare for in-person, phone, and online interviews.
- Provide tips for crafting a professional email message (for emailing potential graduate school advisors, as a thank you after an interview, to inquire about a job, etc.)
- Building in time for role-playing can help students internalize these practices. Students often do not realize how difficult it is to make small talk in a professional setting until they encounter it. Role-playing within a workshop can be a safe, low-stakes opportunity to practice interactions students have just discussed.

Workshop on academic CV/resume writing

This workshop can also be offered to your beginning researchers since many research program applications ask for a CV or resume. As students move through the research process, it is helpful to remind them to continually expand and refine their CVs. Discussion topics can include:

- How to incorporate their research experiences into their CV/resume. Many students will list their retail job experience but not their research or project experience because they don't see these as "real" jobs. Help them see the skills that they've developed in their research projects – time management, ability to handle setbacks, teamwork, etc. – and show them how these can be represented on their CVs and resumes.

• How to incorporate coursework into their CV/resume. Students develop important skills during their courses, it is important to highlight skills relevant to the position (research or job) that they are seeking.

Workshop on funded research opportunities

This workshop introduces students to various ways where they can be paid to conduct research. An overview of the programs and scholarships available at your campus is a good place to start, including any databases your campus may have for these types of opportunities. Students should also be introduced to the extensive list of the National Science Foundation-supported summer Research Experiences for Undergraduates (REUs) opportunities. NSF REUs are mainly for STEM disciplines but can include social science and humanistic social science projects as well. The Big 10 Alliance and the Leadership Alliance both have summer research opportunities for students in all disciplines. Links to these programs are listed in the bullet points below. Summer research experiences are a terrific way for students to get a taste of research, get to know a different institution or even a different part of the country or world, build their resume for graduate school, and receive a stipend. A few items to keep in mind for this workshop:

• Don't assume students know how to apply to research programs – explain how long it takes to apply, what types of materials they need to gather in order to apply, etc.

• Don't assume students have made up their minds to apply – offer encouragement and explain the potential benefits of the experience. A panel of students who have gone through summer research programs or REUs would be helpful here.

• Offer resources for how to find the appropriate funded experience. The National Science Foundation has a searchable website (www.nsf.gov/crssprgm/reu/reu_search.jsp); the Big Ten Summer Research Opportunities Programs (https://btaa.org/resources-for/students/srop/campus-profiles); and the Leadership Alliance (https://theleadershipalliance.org/summer-research-early-identification-program) are just a few excellent places for students to explore. Walking students through some of these websites will also help them feel less overwhelmed when searching for opportunities.

• Explain to students what the different research programs or REUs might be looking for in a successful candidate.

• For some students, especially first-generation college students, the idea of leaving home for 8–10 weeks during the summer can be daunting, and they can face pushback from their families. Offer suggestions for how to cope with this anxiety, emphasizing the benefits of the experience, and provide tips on how to talk to their families about the long-term benefits of this experience.

Workshop on applying to graduate schools

Many students who conduct research as undergraduates will eventually consider attending graduate school. A workshop on the ins and outs of this complicated and lengthy process is extremely helpful to students, especially BIPOC, low-income, and first-generation college students. Some points to consider for this workshop:

- Explain the potential benefits of attending graduate school. A panel of alumni who are currently in graduate programs would be helpful here.
- Explain the differences between master's degrees (MA, MFA, and MS) and Ph.D.
- Review options for paying for a graduate degree. Explain that many disciplines will fully fund a Ph.D. program so students will not need to take out additional loans.
- How to select the appropriate graduate programs to apply to. Many students think that they should apply to all the most well-known institutions. It is important for students to understand that the most well-known institution may not have a strong department or research program in the field they want to study. Provide resources for students to explore potential well-matched graduate programs – faculty mentors, authors of journal articles, etc.
- Help students understand and establish a comprehensive timeline for applications, including time needed to reach out to potential graduate mentors.
- Writing a strong statement of purpose and a strong self-statement, and the differences between the two.
- Provide relevant information for students interested in a variety of disciplines, including humanities and arts.

Final thoughts – remote/in-person/hybrid workshops

There is a wealth of literature and resources on remote learning, but this section will focus on what undergraduate research programs have learned as we have had to transition to remote modalities between 2020 and 2022, and now transition back to a mixture of in-person and remote workshops. In deciding the modality of your workshop, it is worthwhile to consider the goals of the workshop. Is the workshop informational only? Is audience engagement important to achieve the learning objectives? Is the workshop designed for a small subset of your student population or for a broad audience, potentially beyond your campus? Is your campus small and mostly residential or large with a large percentage of commuting students? Having answers to some of these questions will help determine which modality may be most effective in ensuring that the workshop meets its goals.

Although there are several well-known subscription-based online workshop/conference platforms, they are not generally necessary for creating easy to manage and effective online or hybrid workshops. Most campuses have institution-wide subscriptions to online meeting platforms (such as Zoom or those embedded in your learning management system) which can be easily adapted for workshops without extra charge.

In-person only

If the workshop material requires students to interact extensively with the speaker, panel, or each other, in-person workshops are still the best way to engage an audience. On the flip side, in-person workshops usually serve a smaller audience and may exclude those who have unconventional schedules or family obligations. For example, the communication and teamwork workshop we describe earlier, because it requires students to work in multiple small groups, may be more suitable for in-person.

Remote, synchronous

The next best thing to in-person in terms of audience engagement are remote workshops where the speaker and the audience are online at the same time. To ensure student interaction, the speaker or workshop facilitator will need to be very intentional about asking questions through the chat function, use of online polls, use of shared whiteboards, and breakout rooms. This modality allows student participation without requiring that students be on campus – and is thus useful for campuses with many commuting students. However, the synchronous nature will still prevent some students from participating due to work or family obligations.

Remote, synchronous workshops are also great for alumni panels or if you are inviting out-of-state speakers but do not have the budget to pay for travel. We have had great success with hosting graduate school workshops with alumni panels this way. Alumni from all over the country can participate and students generally have found them very engaging. Students often feel less intimidated to ask questions via chat online, as opposed to raising their hands in person.

Hybrid

Hybrid workshops, where the workshop is not only being presented in person but also streamed live to an online audience, require additional support to be effective. Having a support staff to monitor and interact with the online audience will free up the presenter to focus on those attending in-person. However, it may be difficult for the online audience to interact with the in-person audience. Most of the time, the hybrid workshop will feel to the audience like two separate workshops, one in-person, and another online.

Remote, asynchronous

It has been shown that most people only watch the first 5–10 minutes of an online recording. Hence, in designing a remote, asynchronous workshop, it may be useful to create six 5-minute videos as opposed to one 30-minute video. This can be a recorded in-person, hybrid, or remote but synchronous workshop that is made available to a broader audience after the workshop has taken place. Or this can be a recording made specifically to be shared online where the audience can access the recording at any time. This modality has the lowest barrier to audience access but audience interaction is not generally possible. This is well suited for workshops that are mostly informational and audience engagement is not critical. Workshops on CVs/resumes are a good example of content that would be appropriate for this model. Students can view them whenever they are working on their resumes and only watch the portions that they find useful.

Summary

There are multiple ways workshop content can be presented to students. In the most intensive version, students enroll in credit-bearing course(s) with a curriculum of professional development workshops that support them through all stages of their development as researchers, from preparing to apply to their first research experience, through presentation of their research and application to graduate school. Many summer research programs will offer a truncated version of this same curriculum. Finally, these workshops can be offered by your office throughout the academic year to be broadly available on a piecemeal basis.

These workshops are an integral component to the undergraduate research experience, as they help students develop skills that are critical to their success but that may not be part of the actual research experience they are undertaking. Even if your office does not have the staff or potential partnership opportunities across campus to offer the complete curriculum we suggest here, we highly recommend that you provide your students with the resources to participate in these experiences virtually. This will help put the research experience into context in a clear and useful way for students as they move from novice to more experienced researcher.

Notes

1 Strayhorn, T.L. "Satisfaction and Retention Among African American Men at Two-Year Community Colleges." *Community College Journal of Research and Practice*, vol. 36 no. 5, 2012, 358–375.
2 Dong, W., et al. "Effects of Research-Related Activities on Graduation at a Hispanic Serving Institution." *Journal of College Student Retention: Research, Theory & Practice*, vol. 26 no. 1, 2024, 126–150, https://doi.org/10.1177/15210251211065099
3 Priniski, S.J., et al. "The Benefits of Combining Value for the Self and Others in Utility-Value Interventions." *Journal of Educational Psychology*, vol. 111 no. 8, 2019, 1478.
4 Feenstra, S., et al. "Contextualizing the Imposter 'Syndrome'." *Frontiers in Psychology*, vol. 11, 2020, 575024.

References

Dong, W., et al. "Effects of Research-Related Activities on Graduation at a Hispanic Serving Institution." *Journal of College Student Retention: Research, Theory & Practice*, vol. 26 no. 1, 2024, 126–150, https://doi.org/10.1177/15210251211065099
Feenstra, S., et al. "Contextualizing the Imposter 'Syndrome'." *Frontiers in Psychology*, vol. 11, 2020, 575024.
Priniski, S.J., et al. "The Benefits of Combining Value for the Self and Others in Utility-Value Interventions." *Journal of Educational Psychology*, vol. 111 no. 8, 2019, 1478.
Strayhorn, T.L. "Satisfaction and Retention Among African American Men at Two-Year Community Colleges." *Community College Journal of Research and Practice*, vol. 36 no. 5, 2012, 358–375.

7 Facilitating the mentor–mentee relationship

Introduction

There are many mentoring models, all of which focus on the relationship between mentor and mentee. In this chapter, we describe how an office of undergraduate research, scholarship, and creative activity (URSCA) can be an active partner in developing these relationships, as well as how such an office can be an especially powerful ally for students who might not otherwise have developed relationships with, or be comfortable approaching, potential faculty mentors. Mentoring plays an especially important role in ensuring access and inclusion for historically underserved and first-generation students, who may find it challenging to connect with faculty mentors outside the classroom. This may be due to a feeling of intimidation, a sense that they are imposing on faculty time, or because they presume – 99% of the time incorrectly – that they are underqualified for the opportunity. This is in stark contrast to many "traditional" college students who have been found to be more likely to apply for opportunities even when they are not qualified.[1]

To ensure that the positive impact of your office is maximized, it is important to recognize the importance of mentoring as part of your work – to ensure that students are receiving the type of mentorship that can help them be successful. Most people who are engaged in some way with undergraduate research are passionate about student success. They will also come with a variety of professional and personal resources to help students as they navigate the academic, cultural, and personal challenges of entering research culture. Leveraging these relationships within your organization and community is key to making your efforts sustainable and impactful. It is also important to remember that mentoring can come in many forms and from many different types of people, including faculty, staff, postdocs, graduate students, peers, community partners, and other knowledge-bearers.

DOI: 10.4324/9781003154952-7

Inclusive mentoring

Despite evidence showing the impact of research participation on student success measures such as increases in graduation rates and the sense of belonging, BIPOC, low-income, and first-generation students are less likely to participate in undergraduate research compared to their counterparts. Some reasons for the lower levels of undergraduate research participation include less awareness of opportunities, less encouragement from faculty to participate in URSCA, the need to work restricting the amount of time they can devote to research, and the lack of role models/faculty mentors they can identify with.[2] Therefore, it is critical that once students have committed to participating in URSCA, the office of undergraduate research ensures that the mentoring students receive is intentionally inclusive and accessible.

To create an inclusive climate around mentoring it is important to realize that "traditional" research culture can be unwelcoming to many students. Traditionally, undergraduate research is seen as a pathway to graduate studies. The focus on applying to graduate programs naturally excludes many students who are thinking about jobs after graduation. The scheduling of many undergraduate research activities also precludes students who are working or have family obligations from participating. The research environment is also sometimes seen as competitive instead of collaborative, which can be off-putting for many students. To engage as many students as possible, your office can work with faculty mentors on some of the best practices below. We feel that we should start this chapter with a mention of Torie Weiston-Serdan's book *Critical Mentoring: A Practical Guide*,[3] which, while focused on youth mentoring, provides an important critical look at our inherited (though perhaps not examined) mentoring practices and challenges us to examine and update them in order to empower the students we are serving.

Sharing opportunities

A vast majority of students engaged in research were either encouraged by a faculty person or heard about the opportunity through a faculty person. Work with your faculty to understand the impact of their encouragement and reflect upon whom they choose to encourage to participate in undergraduate research and why. Framing research opportunities as a great way to learn more about one's discipline, how research can impact communities, and how research skills can translate to job skills are all effective methods that broaden the appeal of undergraduate research.

Sense of belonging

Social identities shape our academic experiences. BIPOC students revealed that effective mentorship addressed the students' contexts and the inter-connections across those contexts.[4] Safe spaces where all of us can discuss our identities and interests are a crucial part of effective mentoring. Mentors can build trust in their research programs through identifying mutual goals, needs, and priorities. Sharing their own struggles, frustrations, joys, and satisfaction in research with mentees is another way to build trust.

Inclusive mentoring helps students develop a strong sense of disciplinary identity, strong sense of self-efficacy, and tools to navigate within the disciplinary culture. Seeking frequent feedback from students is important, as is validating the different approaches that students might take to a research question based on their educational and personal experiences.

Faculty mentors also need to check their own implicit biases about who and what type of student fits the stereotype of a researcher in their discipline. Help professors take time to reflect on how their own biases and prejudices may affect their mentees and interactions between their mentees. It is important to recognize the negative impact of both stereotype threat and the imposter phenomenon, to encourage mentees to reflect on these feelings, and to provide tools to work with them.

The external environment

For many students from traditionally under-served backgrounds, their social and familial networks are distinct and separate from their research networks. This creates a sense of tension for the students – they feel that the time they spend on research is time taken away from their families and friends. The faculty mentor can help students by creating opportunities for their mentees to get to know one another and building a culture of collaboration and support within their research groups. The faculty mentor can also invite mentees' family and friends to presentations and celebratory events, or help their mentees frame their research in ways that can be understood by their families and the broader community.

Determining the structure of the mentor–mentee relationship

The primary mentor for any student participating in undergraduate research will be the faculty leading the research project, or the principal investigator (PI). Many URSCA offices play the role of matchmaker between mentors and mentees, helping faculty craft reasonable position descriptions and recruiting students to apply. Depending on the staffing structure of your office, you may be able to engage more deeply in this process, actively matching students with a desire to begin research with an appropriate faculty mentor.

The first step in determining the structure for the mentor–mentee relationship is a clear understanding of the project to be undertaken (if project-based), the work the faculty person needs assistance with and for what duration (if faculty-generated), or a general idea of the topic a student would like to investigate (if the project is student-generated). In our offices, we work with potential faculty mentors to generate project/position descriptions to which students can apply.[5] This helps the mentor think through important questions about their project, what role the student can play, and their requirements and expectations for a potential mentee. Because we have staff who are dedicated to this part of the process, we are able to gather and help vet these applications; we highly recommend your office try to be involved at this stage. And if your office does not have staffing to dedicate to this process, a template would be a nice way to guide faculty persons in crafting a sufficiently detailed and inclusive research position description.

Once a mentor–mentee pair has been established, we have found that it is best for them to discuss the structure of their relationship early and continue to reflect on its efficacy and adjust as necessary over the course of the placement. Your office can play an important role in this process by facilitating these conversations, and even providing templates for the mentor–mentee agreement. For mentees, these agreements will usually cover things such as the expectations for how they will connect and communicate with their faculty mentor, grading and other academic requirements, expectations related to research productivity (ranging from timely completion of work, to presentation at disciplinary conferences), as well as any expectations tied to application to additional summer research programs, graduate schools, or jobs, depending on where they are in their research trajectory. Depending on the length and nature of the research placement, the particulars of the mentee side of the agreement may vary.

For mentors, such agreements may be more standardized, but normally include items such as determining a meeting schedule with the mentee, introducing the mentee to the relevant literature and foundational research, expectations for monitoring and guiding the mentee's research, as well as expectations related to dissemination of student research.

In our process, the completed agreement is signed at a meeting in which the student, mentor, and UROC staff review the expectations outlined in the document and discuss the resources and guidance our office provides to assist both mentor and mentees in achieving these goals. If your office does not have the staffing needed to participate actively in these initial mentor–mentee meetings, it is useful to provide a template for such an agreement. Your office can also emphasize the importance for the agreement to be developed as part of a conversation between the faculty person and the student, as opposed to a standard form to sign. The conversation to develop an agreement can look something like this:

Faculty: "I am the kind of mentor who likes to be hands-off so that my mentees feel that they have the room to ask their own questions. How do you feel about that?"

Student: "I like the opportunity to ask my own questions but I usually find that I need specific deadlines for tasks."

or

Student: "I am used to texting with my friends, would that be an appropriate way to communicate my research progress with you?"

Faculty: "I am not comfortable with texting, can we use email instead? I can commit to responding to your emails within 24 hours of receiving them."

Role of the URSCA office

An URSCA office may also want to clarify their own expectations of the mentors they support. At UROC, we developed the following language we both feature on our website and convey in person to all our potential mentors:

> As a UROC mentor you are expected to not only integrate the UROC mentee into your research process and expose them to the research environment, but also to provide them with the direct guidance and scaffolding necessary for a positive learning experience. A good mentor models positive behaviors, fosters a trusting relationship, guides, instructs and motivates the mentee. Additionally, a good mentor continually assesses the mentee's progress to manage expectations and achieve stated goals and objectives while fostering a relationship of mutual respect. UROC mentors help students develop and execute research objectives and learning outcomes that prepare students for advanced study, graduate school, and employment in their field. To that end, mentors will work with their student(s) to complete UROC's Research Planning Guide, which includes project-specific research objectives, learning outcomes, a literature review, and a timeline. Mentors are expected to meet with their student on a predetermined schedule, provide honest and critical feedback to their student, help their student make connections within

the professional community, and aid their student in disseminating results through conference presentations and publications. Mentors will also work closely with UROC Staff to gauge the student's development and progress. We are committed to supporting the development of individualized, rigorous, and creative action plans.

Mentor training

Becoming a good or even great mentor takes work. There are varying cultures of mentoring across disciplines, and most of us will not have had any formal training in mentorship. As such, we encourage your office to familiarize yourself with best practices and to consider developing opt-in mentor training workshops, especially for new faculty mentors and graduate student mentors.[6] Developing a healthy mentor–mentee relationship will require some or all of the following from mentors.

Reflection

No two mentors are exactly alike and there is no perfect mentor, but through reflection, everyone can serve as a great mentor. It is important for mentors to take stock of their own communication preferences, strengths and weaknesses, personal experiences as a mentor and a mentee, and potential unconscious biases to develop a mentoring philosophy. Mentors should know why they choose to mentor students in undergraduate research, what they hope to gain from the experience, and what they hope their mentees will gain. A good resource for this activity can be found on the website of the University of Colorado, Boulder, Undergraduate Research Opportunities Program website: www.colorado.edu/urop/mentoring-guide/reflect-and-plan

Understanding your mentees

No two mentees are exactly alike, what works for one may not work well for another. By taking the time to get to know the mentees in the beginning of the mentor–mentee relationship, the mentor can avoid misunderstandings, unrealistic expectations, and other relationship pitfalls. Some good topics to discuss with mentees include: What does the mentee hope to get out of the experience? What are the mentee's educational and career goals? Are there potential barriers that the mentee can foresee that would make it difficult to meet the requirements of a research project? What are the mentee's communication preferences?

Establishing expectations

While we have covered some of this in the section on mentor–mentee agreements above, this advice is geared toward the mentor who may not have the benefit of the formal structures we describe. Once the basic motivations of the mentor and the mentee have been explored, it is important to establish expectations of the mentor–mentee relationship. These expectations are best discussed in-person with the mentee, offering opportunities for the mentee to weigh in on whether the mentor's expectations match the mentee's and whether the expectations are feasible. (It is ok to set high expectations as long as the mentee knows that the mentor is there to support them to reach those expectations! It is also ok for the expectations to change as a response to the mentee's growth and changing needs.) It is advisable for the expectations to be documented and shared between the mentor and the mentee. Resources for documenting mentor–mentee expectations include this resource from the Center for Engaged Learning at Elon University on setting clear and well-scaffolded expectations: www.centerforengagedlearning.org/salientpractices/setting-clear-and-well-scaffolded-expectations/, and from the UROP program at the University of Colorado, Boulder, advice on creating a mentor agreement: www.colorado.edu/urop/mentoring-guide/create-mentor-agreement

Acknowledgment and motivation

Mentees are people and people need to be acknowledged when they are working in challenging situations. Acknowledgment is not cheerleading or offering platitudes, but actions or statements that show the mentee that their efforts and accomplishments – regardless of how small – are seen. Mentors can respond in the moment to something the mentee said or did, such as "I hear what you are saying and I am thinking about it," "I saw how uncomfortable those questions made you feel and here are some things we can do in the future," "It is evident that you put a lot of effort into the current draft of the report," "I shared with you my comments about your research, what are your thoughts?," etc. The concept of acknowledgment can also be extended to the mentees' background and experience. Acknowledgment is one, often overlooked, aspect of motivating mentees to go above and beyond. Other factors in motivation include providing mentees with meaning, pride, challenge, and ownership over what they are doing.

Mentoring is messy

Because every mentor is different and every mentee is different, the relationship doesn't always work out – and that is ok. No one mentor can meet a mentee's every need. Mentors can introduce their mentees to additional potential mentors, including another student (peer mentor), another faculty member, a staff member, or someone in industry who may have the background or expertise that the mentee is seeking. In the case where a mentoring relationship needs to end, the mentor should leave open the opportunity to connect again in the future, for example, "Although we will no longer be working together on this project, I look forward to supporting you in your academic/professional journey. Please let me know how I can continue to support you."

Mentee support

The research mentor–mentee relationship is often a student's first experience with a mentor. As such, it is helpful for students to understand what it means to have a mentor, the potential benefits, and actions they can take to get the most out of that relationship. Some of the best practices include the following (these can go into a formal mentoring agreement if your office has the capacity to develop and manage that process).

Develop common expectations

It is important to understand what the mentor expects and to think about one's own goals for the mentoring relationship. Students should think about why they want a mentor and what they hope to get out of the relationship. Some examples of outcomes may be a letter of recommendation for a job or graduate school; to be a named author on a publication from the research project; guidance on how to conduct research; building a broader professional network; etc. Students should let their mentors know about their goals and understand that mentors appreciate knowing how they can better help their mentees succeed. Students should also ask mentors about mentor expectations. Example questions are "How often should we meet and for how long?," "What should I prepare to share with you during our meetings?," and "What deliverables (reports, presentations, etc.) do you expect from me at the end of this project?"

Be prepared

Mentors are busy and have limited time; being prepared means the student will be able to get the most out of the time they spend with their mentor. Students should take the time to prepare for every meeting – results they want to share with their mentor, questions about their current progress, questions about the direction of the research, questions about their career path, etc. Questions for mentors should be ones that relate to the mentor and not general questions that can be easily searched for online.

Ask for feedback, show appreciation

Mentors are there to help students succeed. Students can make sure they are benefiting from having a mentor by asking for feedback. Example questions include "Am I meeting your expectations for progress on this project?" and "What else can I be doing to be more prepared for my career goals?" Students can show appreciation for the mentor's time by following through on the mentor's recommendations and reporting back on results of the follow-through. Following through shows the mentors that students are taking their advice seriously and value the mentor's perspectives.

It is ok to have more than one mentor

No one mentor can meet a mentee's every need. If a student feels that there are aspects where their current mentor is not able to assist, they should ask their mentor to introduce them to other mentors. Example queries include "I would love to get a job at [name of company] when I graduate. Do you have any contacts at [name of company] that you can introduce me to?," "I would love to talk to other students who have similar backgrounds as me. Would you be able to introduce me to other students or alumni you feel can mentor me?," and "I am also interested in exploring topics in [name of] field. Can you recommend a faculty member that I can talk to about [proposed field]?"

Program considerations

The above are examples of support your office can provide to mentors and mentees in general. For offices providing mentor–mentee pairing either as a stand-alone service or in conjunction with grant-funded research opportunities, these are additional elements to consider.

Faculty mentor selection

Consider the diversity of your mentor pool while being conscious of whether BIPOC faculty mentors are asked to do an inordinate amount of mentoring. To ensure a healthy faculty mentor pool, stay in touch with potential faculty mentors and provide frequent trainings or workshops on mentoring best practices.

Maintenance

Provide a mechanism for students and faculty to let the program know when a mentor–mentee relationship is not working. Conduct periodic check-in's with faculty and students to catch small problems before they develop into big ones. Develop procedures for what to do if problems cannot be resolved between a student and a faculty mentor. It is important to identify effective mentors and highlight their best practices. It is equally important to identify problematic mentors through student feedback or outcomes.

Length of placement

Consider offering projects that have shorter engagement periods, especially for students who are new to research. Although traditional research relationships last at least one academic term to multiple years, these types of research apprenticeships may not be feasible for students who are not convinced that research is for them, for students who have other obligations, or for other non-traditional students. Having a few options for students to engage in experiential learning with faculty mentors for a few days or a few weeks can increase the students' confidence and commitment to longer-term research relationships.

Summary

Even if you are beginning as an office of one, we highly recommend spending the time to determine how your office will support the development of a healthy mentor-mentee relationship. This can be as simple as having a resource list for mentors. Resources could include examples of learning outcomes based on the educational level of the mentees, best practices for working in a team, best practices in equitable and inclusive mentoring, etc. We recommend the following to start:

- Shanahan, J.O., et al. "Ten Salient Practices of Undergraduate Research Mentors: A Review of the Literature." *Mentoring & Tutoring: Partnership in Learning*, vol. 5, 2015, 359–376, https://doi.org/10.1080/13611267.2015.1126162
- Weiston-Serdan, T. *Critical Mentoring: A Practical Guide*. Routledge, 2017, www.routledge.com/Critical-Mentoring-A-Practical-Guide/Weiston-Serdan/p/book/9781620365526
- The Council on Undergraduate Research also maintains a resource library that you can access with a CUR individual or institutional membership: www.cur.org/engage/mentors/

Though the following may take greater capacity, we also recommend providing workshops, discussion groups, and other resources for mentors to connect with other mentors and access best practices. A good place to start when developing these resources is the Leadership Alliance.[7] On the resources section of their website (https://theleadershipalliance.org/resources), they offer articles on mentoring, unconscious bias, post-baccalaureate and career options, and teaching. Additionally, they have developed mentoring guides for research in both STEM, and Humanities and Social Sciences. Zia Isola and Malika Bell of UC Santa Cruz developed a Mentoring 101: essential skills module that can be used with groups of faculty mentors as they consider their roles, and responsibilities as research mentors. (The presentation can be accessed here: https://bpb-us-e1.wpmucdn.com/sites. ucsc.edu/dist/b/1275/files/2017/05/MentorWorkshop2013_0.pdf)   Lastly, two sample mentor–mentee agreements are included at the conclusion of this chapter, following the vignette from the California Institute of Technology (Caltech) describing how they support their research mentors.

VIGNETTE 7.1   Mentoring at Caltech

Candace Rypisi, Assistant Vice Provost and
Director of Student–Faculty Programs at
California Institute of Technology

Caltech is a small, private science and engineering school in Pasadena, California. We have 1,000 undergraduates, 1,400 graduate students, and 300 faculty. Research is a core component of the undergraduate experience. Over 90% of students participate in at least one research project before they graduate. Most students do this through the Summer Undergraduate Research Fellowships (SURF) program that began in 1979. SURF is modeled on the grant-seeking process:

- Students collaborate with a potential mentor to define and develop a project.
- Applicants write a research proposal as part of the application process.
- A faculty committee reviews proposals and recommend awards.
- Students submit two interim reports, an abstract, a final paper, and give an oral presentation at SURF Seminar Day, symposia modeled on a professional technical meeting.

Effective mentoring is critical to student learning and ensuring a positive experience. Each year we have approximately 225 faculty mentors and an additional 250 co-mentors. Co-mentors are the graduate students and postdoctoral fellows who provide much of the day-to-day oversight of undergraduate researchers.

In 2015, Student–Faculty Programs (SFPs), the office that administers the SURF program, and Caltech's Center for Teaching, Learning, and Outreach (CTLO), conducted a survey of co-mentors to better understand their preparation to serve as a research mentor. We found that nearly 40% of the respondents were first-time co-mentors and 90% had never participated in any mentoring-related professional development. In response to our findings, we designed a nine-hour competency-based workshop series adapted from the *Entering Mentoring* (Pfund et al., 2014) curriculum. Workshops focused on six core mentoring competencies: aligning expectations; assessing understanding; maintaining effective communication; addressing diversity; fostering independence; and promoting professional development. We enhanced the workshops with content on student development, learning theory, and key diversity concepts. Approximately 25–30 co-mentors participate each year. In subsequent pre- and post-surveys, participants have reported gains in each competency and feel more prepared to mentor undergraduate researchers.

One piece of important feedback was that some co-mentors expressed interest in the workshops but could not commit to the six-week program. In 2016, we launched an annual day-long conference that provided introductory information on each of the core mentoring competencies. Each year the conference has a new theme (mentoring across difference; building your mentoring toolkit, activating your mentoring superpowers, etc.) and is comprised of panel discussions with senior mentors and/or undergraduate mentees; small group discussions based on research area; competency-based workshops; and a plenary speaker. The conference attracts 75–125 participants a year.

Due to the interest in this topic, we have also launched a Certificate of Interest in Undergraduate Research Mentoring. Participants must attend at least six seminars or workshops, submit a reflection journal entry on what they've learned, and write a personal mentoring philosophy.

Collectively these efforts have helped increase the level of effective mentoring provided to our undergraduate researchers while supporting the professional development of our future faculty.

Sample mentor agreement

Undergraduate Research Opportunities Center,
California State University, Monterey Bay

The Faculty Mentor plays a critical role in the UROC/MacNair Scholars Program. The Scholar's success depends on an effective Mentor–Scholar relationship. The Faculty Mentor's goals are to develop the Scholar's confidence, research skills, communication skills, knowledge of ethical conduct in research, professional networking skills, and critical thinking abilities. To accomplish these goals, Faculty Mentors will:

1. Meet regularly with the Scholar following a predetermined meeting schedule.
2. Alert UROC staff at the first sign of academic, programmatic, or personal difficulties (such as missed meetings or late assignments). As appropriate, work with UROC staff to develop an intervention strategy.
3. Introduce the Scholar to foundational research in their field. Identify scholarly work for the Scholar to review and work with the Scholar to develop their research interests. Recommended deliverable: Literature review or research introduction.
4. Assist the Scholar with developing a Research Planning Guide.
5. Monitor and, as appropriate, guide the research process.*
6. Assist the Scholar in preparing research posters, oral presentations, and/or peer-reviewed publications.
7. Help the Scholar identify and apply for undergraduate scholarships, funding for undergraduate research, graduate school programs, and graduate school funding opportunities, as appropriate.
8. Review and sign the Mentor agreement.
9. Monitor and assess the Scholar's Individual Learning Plan to ensure that it is in line with requirements for graduate study within the Scholar's intended field of study.
10. Acknowledge UROC. During the course of their undergraduate research activities, UROC participants may be supported directly and indirectly by multiple grants stemming from UROC. We ask that Faculty Mentors acknowledge any and all support provided by UROC when they and/or their students disseminate results

of their research (including poster presentations, oral presentations, peer-reviewed publications, grey/white papers, etc.). To this end, we request that you visit the UROC Mentor FAQ webpage https://csumb.edu/uroc/mentor-faqs for more information about acknowledging UROC support and/or email UROC uroc@csumb.edu with any questions or concerns.

*This section will vary depending on whether this agreement addresses a faculty- or student-generated project, or if the student is joining an ongoing research group or lab.

Sample mentor–mentee agreement

Office of Undergraduate Research, Cal Poly Pomona

Mentor and mentee agreement

A key element to a productive and rewarding mentor–mentee relationship is clear communication of expectations. This agreement is intended to serve as a guideline to facilitate communications between faculty mentors and their scholar. This document should be reviewed and completed by the faculty mentor and scholar jointly, and we recommended for this to be completed at the first meeting between the faculty mentor and scholar (in-person or virtually).

Sections from this agreement have been adapted from the CAL-BRIDGE Faculty Mentor–Scholar Mentorship Agreement.

To help kick off your research mentor–mentee relationship, please complete the following:

General Expectations

Mentor (please describe your general expectations for your mentee, what do you hope the mentee will accomplish, what do you hope the mentee will learn, what deliverables do you expect by the end of the research period?) _____

_____

Mentee (please describe your general expectations for this research period, what do you hope to learn, what do you expect to accomplish by the end of the research period, and what are your expectations of your faculty mentor?) _____

_____

Communication

Mentor and mentee, please complete the following together: mode of communication, select all that apply

__ Phone (insert numbers): _____

__ Email (insert email addresses): _____

__ CPP email (if applicable): _____

__ Text (insert numbers): _____

__ Other platform (insert platform): _____

How quickly should the mentee expect the mentor to respond? _____ (weekday vs. weekend)

How quickly should the mentor expect the mentee to respond? _____ (weekday vs. weekend)

__ The scholar acknowledges that they will update faculty mentor and STARS/SURE Program Staff with progress as appropriate. Any struggles either academically or with program requirements will be brought forward and discussed in a timely manner.

Meetings

Who will be responsible for scheduling the meetings? _____

Mentor (please complete the following):

Frequency of meetings:_____

Mode of meetings (in-person/online/both):_____
_____

Type of meetings (team/individual): _____

What should the mentee bring to the meeting or send ahead of each meeting? _____

What do you expect to be discussed at each meeting? _____
_____

What should the mentee do if they need to be late to or miss a meeting? _____

What will I do if I need be late to or miss a meeting? _____

Mentor, please complete the following:

I will strive to be supportive, equitable, accessible, encouraging, and respectful by _____

(suggestions for above – asking the mentee about their professional goals and help them reach those goals; modeling and encouraging respectful behavior; providing resources for mentees to be successful; fostering professional confidence by providing constructive feedback; advocating for the mentee; etc.)

Mentee, please complete the following:

I will strive to contribute to a supportive, equitable, accessible, encouraging, and respectful environment by_____

(suggestions for above – treating everyone with respect; letting the mentor know if there are issues in the lab or the research group; being encouraging to other members of the lab or research group; communicating my professional goals with the mentor; being open to constructive feedback; etc.)

Time to respond to feedback

Mentor: I commit to providing feedback on

Conference abstracts that are submitted to me ___ days before the due date.
Posters and presentations that are submitted to me ___ days before the due date.
Reports and papers that are submitted to me ___ days before the due date.

Notes

1 Aikens, M.L., et al. "Race and Gender Differences in Undergraduate Research Mentoring Structures and Research Outcomes." *CBE—Life Sciences Education,* vol. 16 no. 2, 2017, ar34.
2 Haeger, H., et al. "Creating More Inclusive Research Environments for Undergraduates." *Journal of the Scholarship of Teaching and Learning,* vol. 21 no. 1, 2021.
3 Weiston-Serdan, T. *Critical Mentoring: A Practical Guide.* Routledge, 2017.
4 Chan, A.W., et al. "Mentoring Ethnic Minority Counseling and Clinical Psychology Students: A Multicultural, Ecological, and Relational Model." *Journal of Counseling Psychology,* vol. 62 no. 4, 2015, 592–607, https://doi.org/10.1037/cou0000079
5 At CSUMB, we utilize a simple Google form to gather this information, which can be accessed here: https://docs.google.com/forms/d/e/1FAIpQLSe2XNEDv

77FT0fvZ1TF2UD3xUHyNM_875iCjulo7s44NVBbXQ/viewform,   Cal   Poly
Pomona uses a similar form: https://forms.office.com/r/P0gpTYXTcd
6 We should note that on our own campuses, we have found that faculty are much
more likely to participate in mentor training programs if they are not *called* mentor training: we have had success with session/workshop titles like "Getting the
most out of your mentee."
7 The leadership alliance is a partnership of 35 institutions that have come together
to offer resources to develop underrepresented students into outstanding leaders
and role models in academia, business, and the public sector.

References

Aikens, M.L., et al. "Race and Gender Differences in Undergraduate Research
Mentoring Structures and Research Outcomes." *CBE—Life Sciences Education*,
vol. 16 no. 2, 2017, ar34.
Chan, A.W., et al. "Mentoring Ethnic Minority Counseling and Clinical Psychol-
ogy Students: A Multicultural, Ecological, and Relational Model." *Journal of
Counseling Psychology*, vol. 62 no. 4, 2015, 592–607.
Haeger, H., et al. "Creating More Inclusive Research Environments for Undergrad-
uates." *Journal of the Scholarship of Teaching and Learning*, vol. 21 no. 1, 2021.
Pfund, C., et al. "Training Mentors of Clinical and Translational Research Scholars:
A Randomized Controlled Trial." *Academic Medicine*, vol. 89 no. 5, 2014, 774–782.

8 Top down, bottom up: tenure, promotion, and other faculty and mentor support strategies

Participation in undergraduate research can be a memorable, life-altering experience for both students and faculty alike, especially when it aligns with academic requirements. However, for faculty – especially junior faculty on the tenure-track – incorporating undergraduates into a research agenda may prove to be challenging, depending on how well they are supported by their department/college. This is where the assistance of your fledgling undergraduate research office can be critical. Meetings and discussions with Deans, Chairs, and faculty can be a productive means of brainstorming and generating support for ways in which your campus can encourage and incentivize faculty participation in undergraduate research. Apart from the usual monetary/financial incentives, colleges can think about creative ways in which faculty may be rewarded for involving undergraduates in their research, taking care to ensure these rewards align with tenure and promotion metrics established by the college. In cases where faculty have the freedom to develop and teach Course-based Undergraduate Research Experiences (CUREs, see Chapter 12), there may be some rich, synergistic overlap between their teaching and student research mentoring activities.

Incentives and encouragement

In our experience, different faculty are motivated by different reasons to engage undergraduates in their research. Some faculty immediately see the merits of incorporating students into their laboratories or studios, relishing the chance to hone their mentoring skills while boosting their research productivity. This is often especially the case on campuses where undergraduate teaching is highly valued – faculty see mentoring undergraduate research as a clear strategy for success that aligns well with the campus vision and mission. In units where faculty get workload credit for supervising undergraduate research, the message that this important work is valued

DOI: 10.4324/9781003154952-8

gets multiplied; some faculty may further be motivated by the prospect of course buyouts stemming from their mentoring work. In other cases, faculty may be more motivated by the opportunity to get extra financial resources – in the form of either summer salary or research support for students. Of course, many faculty are motivated by all of the above. Whatever the motivation, when you are starting up a center, you'll want to identify all of the possible means of support that might motivate faculty – and then rank them in order of importance. Ideally, again, your center would offer a host of incentives from which faculty could choose – but practically speaking this is often not possible.

Special consideration should be given to supporting faculty mentors at different stages of their careers. For early career tenure-track faculty, there should ideally be a clear connection between their undergraduate research mentoring activities and their tenure and promotion goals. This is where having your undergraduate research staff working with Chairs, Associate Deans, and Deans of different colleges will be invaluable. Strategically planning for how to "have a seat at the table" when discussions of tenure and promotion policy are occurring should be part of your research center development scheme. Having a senior faculty or administrative center director can boost your chances of being involved in these important discussions. Being an active participant in faculty senate activities/deliberations may also be an important strategic move.

Finally, there will always be faculty who decline to work with your center to engage undergraduates in research. In our experience, sometimes this can be overcome with a little outreach – not all faculty realize that there is support for them to mentor students (especially in some disciplines that do not have a strong tradition of undergraduate involvement in research/scholarly activities). Even within STEM, we have encountered faculty who do not believe students should be or can be involved in research while undergraduates, but rather should wait until graduate school. In a few notable cases, this perspective came from faculty in the mathematical sciences who suggested that undergraduates were not equipped to undertake research because of the pyramidal nature of knowledge in pure mathematics; that is, students need to wait until they have four years of foundational mathematics under their belts to make any kind of meaningful contribution. You may encounter similar arguments from faculty in the Humanities, where there is also a strong culture of single-scholar authorship. You might suggest, in such situations, that there are myriad applications of, for example, mathematics that are suitable for collaboration with undergraduates. Indeed, undergraduates often develop a love for mathematics only after immersing in applications that hold deep meaning for them. In any case, open and transparent discussions about differences in perspectives across the disciplines are likely to be part of the process.

Mentor compensation and recognition

Another large challenge you will have to tackle is the question of mentor compensation: to pay faculty or not? This can be a contentious issue, with some chairs and administrators arguing that faculty (especially tenure-track faculty) are already being paid to teach and mentor undergraduates and should not expect extra compensation for helping their students engage in research – especially if it benefits their own research productivity! On the other hand, many faculty and administrators understand that, in today's higher education climate, faculty are becoming overwhelmed with so many responsibilities that extra compensation (especially when they are off-contract in the summer) can keep them engaged and raise morale. See Vignette 8.1 from the Appalachian College Association for a range of illustrative strategies for engaging/incentivizing faculty involvement.

Regardless of what you decide about remuneration, it's important to recognize the valuable work contributed by mentors. An annual undergraduate research mentor award can showcase exemplary mentoring work while also highlighting excellent outcomes stemming from your undergraduate research program. At CSUMB, for instance, we celebrate our Mentor of the Year by presenting them with a monetary award and a small engraved trophy at a year-end event that also celebrates student achievements. Incorporating this type of mentor recognition into your annual programming can boost faculty interest in participating in undergraduate research as well as provide a CV line item to help with retention and tenure processes.

Academic credit vs. pay: students vs. faculty?

An unintended consequence of incentive programs that is worth considering as you develop your center/office is the potential collision of faculty mentoring incentives provided by departments, and compensation that your research center is offering to both faculty and students. First, in cases where faculty are given credit by their departments toward course buy-outs for supervising internships and research experiences for undergraduates, you or the department chairs/Dean may not want to offer faculty additional compensation for mentoring, as this might be considered "double-dipping." In cases where credit is offered for research-based activities, having some sort of research ("R") designation associated with the course credit can be a terrific way to keep track of student participation in authentic research activities as well as easily track data for assessing outcomes (for one example, see Vignette 8.2, from the University of Washington Tacoma). Some research centers opt for a flexible approach, offering students either academic credit or a stipend/scholarship for their undergraduate research efforts. That said, some academic units hold a dim view of offering students both academic credit and stipends to conduct undergraduate research. Taken together, these complications may result in you asking faculty to choose between having their students sign up for research credits (in order for the faculty member to get supervisory credit with their department) and offering stipends to the students for research activities. In our experience, these arrangements are best tailored to the needs of students and faculty mentors on a case-by-case basis.[1] Needless to say, early and frequent communication among all parties involved, along with a willingness to be flexible, are critical. We find that regular meetings with Deans, along with mentor intake meetings with students and faculty aimed at setting expectations, are invaluable.

VIGNETTE 8.1

Dr. Beth Rushing, President, Appalachian College Association

The Appalachian College Association is a consortium of 34 private colleges and universities in Appalachia. Our institutions are primarily rural and serve significant proportions of low-income students. Most of our schools are small (median FTE is about 1,000) and faculty have higher instructional loads than at larger, better-resourced institutions. All of the institutions in our consortium prioritize teaching effectiveness in faculty evaluation, but they also have expectations for scholarly and creative activity.

One way that our consortium supports faculty-mentored undergraduate research is through an endowed fund that allows us to offer small grants for faculty-sponsored research for Appalachian students. The Colonel Lee B. Ledford Scholars program has funded over 500 projects (exceeding $1.5 million) since the program's inception in 2004. Most of the funding for this program goes to the student researcher; we have used different strategies for incentivizing faculty mentors with stipends or other relatively small awards. We always make sure to recognize the faculty mentors in publicity about the awards and in notes to their campus presidents and academic leaders. Many of these projects have resulted in presentations at professional conferences, and several of our student researchers have published the results of their work in peer-reviewed publications. Even when the faculty incentives for supervising Ledford Scholars' research are minimal, faculty members have expressed eagerness to mentor their students' work.

Faculty-sponsored undergraduate research is valued at each of our consortium's institutions, in different ways that reflect institutional mission, resources, and curriculum. Here are a few examples of the interplay of these elements:

- Young Harris College has identified "Undergraduate Research for the Common Good" as the focus of its institutional accreditation quality enhancement plan. Faculty receive stipends to manage both Course-based Undergraduate Research Experiences and mentored research experiences. In addition, faculty supervision of undergraduate research is counted as part of the scholarship component of faculty evaluation procedures such as tenure and promotion. The commitment to faculty-led undergraduate research is also exemplified in its award for the best faculty mentor, bestowed at the annual Undergraduate Research Day.
- Tennessee Wesleyan University offers competitive research grants for faculty to engage in course-based research, as a component of its institutional focus on using high-impact practices to link educational experiences to future career goals. They are exploring other avenues for creating additional incentives for mentoring undergraduate research.
- At Maryville College, undergraduate research and creative expression is a graduation requirement. Every student completes a Senior Study in their major field, guided by a faculty member. Performance as a faculty mentor in these projects is a component of each faculty members' evaluation.
- Berea College has a program that offers faculty a stipend and budget for working with undergraduates for summer research. The Undergraduate Research and Creative Projects Program funds projects in STEM fields as well as social science, arts, and humanities. Supervision of student research and creative projects is encouraged for Berea faculty but is not in itself sufficient to satisfy the scholarly expectations for tenure and promotion there.

The Appalachian College Association has been an enthusiastic supporter of our member institutions' undergraduate research initiatives. We are currently planning a series of programs that will provide support for both faculty members and campus academic leaders (chairs, Deans, and Provosts) to improve processes and programs for faculty-mentored undergraduate research.

VIGNETTE 8.2   Resources to support faculty and undergraduate research at the University of Washington Tacoma

Cheryl Greengrove, Ph.D., Associate Vice-Chancellor
for Research and Associate Professor of Geoscience

University of Washington Tacoma (UWT) was established in 1990 as a new campus of the University of Washington and initially designed to provide access to the last two years of a public higher education undergraduate degree for non-traditional, place-bound and time-bound students. At the time, Washington State had a robust community college system but limited seats at public universities where students could complete their undergraduate degrees. UWT was one of five new campuses in Washington State created for this purpose. Over time, these campuses added graduate programs and in 2006 expanded to include all four years of an undergraduate curriculum. Today, UWT is a community engaged, urban, and minority-serving institution with a diverse, primarily undergraduate student population, 54% of whom are the first in their families to go to college, 63% students of color, and 16% military affiliated, as well as a large population of transfer students.

Along with its teaching focus, a key part of the UWT mission is to "Foster scholarship, research and creativity to address the challenging problems of our time and place."[2] Research is a key component of the tenure and promotion process, and faculty are strongly encouraged, but not required, to seek funding for their research. Community-engaged scholarship, interdisciplinary research, applied, use-inspired research with public impact, as well as research and scholarship of teaching and involvement of undergraduates in research are all recognized and valued.

Some of the infrastructure and resources available to faculty to support their research and scholarship at UWT include a central campus Office of Research (OR) designed to help principal investigators develop proposals for both internal and external sources of funding. In addition, an Office of Community Partnerships was established at UWT to encourage community-engaged scholarship and promote community collaboration.

There are several internal sources of funds for research available UW-wide, as well as at the local campus level, including the Royalty Research Fund (RRF) supporting faculty research with grants up to $40,000, the Population Health Initiative funding pilot grants to enhance interdisciplinary collaborations between faculty and the community to address critical challenges to population health, EarthLab funding innovation grants supporting an equitable and sustainable world of research, Global Affairs funding for transformative cross-college, cross-continent research collaborations, and Simpson Center for Humanities funding. There are also UW-wide funds available to support undergraduate research, including funds to support student travel to conferences and participation in the annual UW Seattle Undergraduate Research Symposium.

Locally at UWT, incorporating high-impact teaching practices, such as experiential learning and involving students in undergraduate research are highly encouraged. About six years ago, UW implemented an R designation for courses that contained an authentic research component. At that time, UWT formed an Undergraduate Community of Practice group which framed a document outlining the requirements for an R course designation and presented examples of existing ways undergraduate students are involved in research on campus. Current opportunities for undergraduates to engage in research include a Course-based Undergraduate Research Experience (CURE) – a regular course with an embedded substantial research project (typically in STEM majors) – a capstone or senior thesis course often required by a major, or independent study with a faculty mentor for credit. In addition, students often continue working with faculty mentors while being paid on research grants (most frequently in the STEM fields), which often leads to students co-authoring publications.

UWT internal funding to support faculty research more broadly comes from the Founders Endowment Fund designated for academically related activities like curriculum development and research. Support for research from these funds is typically on the order of $40,000 per year which is distributed through an application process run by the faculty Research Advisory Committee. The Office of Community Partnerships also has a limited number of $10,000 grants issued to teams involved in research with community partners. To support junior faculty research, UWT has implemented a research quarter for tenure-track faculty between their third and fifth year prior to going up for tenure, and sabbaticals are available through an application process for all faculty every seven years. The primary source of funding for research continues to come from externally funded grants, predominantly in the STEM fields. In fiscal year 2023, faculty wrote 88 proposals, 48 of which were funded for a total of $11.8 million dollars of extramural funding, a new record for the campus.

Notes

1 We should note again that we encourage campuses to pay their students whenever possible, as this is an important component of making participation in
  URSCA equitable.
2 UWT webpage: www.tacoma.uw.edu/home/vision-mission-and-values

9 Navigating institutional bureaucracy: risk management, research supplies, travel, and other administrative concerns

There is a great deal of administrative work that comes along with running any campus office. This chapter will focus on the nuts and bolts of student research placement, including mentor agreements and compensation, risk management, providing for research supplies, negotiating student travel, and basics of student information management. We will also discuss how to advocate for your program needs and managing administrative expectations through rich and poor times.

Understanding your institutional bureaucracy

First things first, the more you understand your institution, and the people behind it, the more effective you will be. Are you part of a public institution that uses state funds? What regulations are there for expending state funds? Does your institution have private funding, what regulations govern those? Do you have federal grants? Who are the people that approve the use of these various funding sources? Are the rules strictly enforced or is there room to request exceptions?

Who do you report to and do they have budgetary authority for your office? What is the process for requesting support for your office? Who does your boss report to? What are the institutional priorities and how does your office align with those priorities?

Who are the people that get things done in each division? Is there someone in Human Resources that you can call when the hiring process gets stuck? Cultivating relationships with key personnel can go a long way in helping you navigate institutional bureaucracy – this means being respectful to the people you work with and try not to let your frustration with the bureaucracy overflow to the people who are trying to help you with it. The first part of this chapter will walk you through items to consider when working through your institutional bureaucracy.

DOI: 10.4324/9781003154952-9

Student research placements

Placing your students with your faculty

If your office will assist with student research placements on your own campus, there are some things to consider. First, are there faculty who already run research labs who might have the interest and capacity to mentor one or more undergraduate students? If so, will the faculty person serve as the primary mentor, or will there be a graduate student or postdoc in the lab who will share in some of this work? Working with undergraduates, for whom this may be a very new experience, may require some recalibration of expectations. Be sure to address questions such as required safety training, responsible conduct of research, and working in teams and more with your faculty person prior to arranging student placement in their lab. Especially if they are accustomed to working with more advanced mentees, they may need to adjust expectations and provide additional training in lab protocols prior to commencing work with the student (mentor–mentee agreements are discussed in more detail in Chapter 7).

Outside of the STEM disciplines, it is far less common for faculty to have an ongoing research lab or project which students might join. Arranging research, scholarship, or creative activity placements for students in the arts, humanities, or social sciences will require a different approach as a result, and your office may need to do some more nuanced matchmaking to find the right fit between faculty and student mentee. As our offices have expanded beyond their original, grant-funded, STEM foci, we have found that there are a couple of ways we can work to ensure equitable opportunities for students in disciplines where working in a lab is not part of the research culture. We spend a good deal of time connecting with faculty (at new faculty orientations, in departmental and divisional meetings, and even one-on-one as time permits) to describe what our office does and our desire to work with them to help shape opportunities for students to undertake original research. We explain that this can happen either as part of a project they are working on or, more often, how they can mentor a student in an area the student is interested in, even if it is not exactly within their area of expertise.

We have also found that it is important that our office provides support for students who may have an original research idea or area or scholarly interest they would like to pursue, but don't know how to go about finding or approaching a potential mentor. We will meet with these students and help them shape a preliminary idea, identify potential on-campus mentors, and offer advice on how to approach those faculty to see if they might be willing (and a good fit) to serve as a research mentor.

Again, the degree to which you will be able to engage in the research placement process will be highly dependent upon your staffing levels, and where you have decided to direct the majority of your own and your staff's time. We recommend that your office develop a basic understanding of how both faculty and students can receive either academic credit or funding/compensation for this work, even if you will not administer the funding or paperwork yourself. Your ability to guide both parties through the administrative hurdles will make you an exceptionally valuable partner.

Placing external students with your faculty

This most often occurs during summer research programs where you bring students from external institutions to your campus. In addition to some of the concerns we address above, in this scenario, you should also:

- Consult your risk management office to determine whether the external students are covered under your institution's umbrella insurance.
- Consult your risk management office to determine what types of waivers the students need to sign.
- Consult your IT office to provide external students access to software, campus buildings, library resources, online resources that the faculty mentors may require students to use for their research, etc.
- Notify your student health center and psychological services center so that they know these students are on your campus and may need support.

Placing your students with external mentors

For smaller campuses, especially those with a teaching (i.e., not research) mission, the opportunities for your students will be increased exponentially if you build relationships with local research, historical, and cultural institutions. The California State University system has become much more research-focused over the last decade, but when the CSU Monterey Bay UROC office was first formalized, there were few organized research labs on our campus. The regional partnerships we developed at that time remain integral parts of our program even as our campus grows. Even at a large research-focused campus, it may be best to look for external summer research opportunities for your students, whether in formal REUs, or in individually brokered placements for students who come from disciplines where such opportunities do not exist. Regardless of whether the external mentor works at a corporation, another university, or at a federal lab, you will need to do the following:

- Distinguish between an internship and a research assistantship. Typically, different offices oversee different student experiences. Your institution may already have a co-op office or internship office. We have found that the following description helps differentiate between internship and research experiences: Internships are defined as supervised, career-related work experiences leading to the development of knowledge, skills, and abilities needed in a particular profession. Internships may also be related to research, education, or outreach activities.[1] As noted elsewhere in this document, we rely on the Council on Undergraduate Research (CUR)'s definition of undergraduate research, "a mentored investigation or creative inquiry conducted by an undergraduate that seeks to make a scholarly or artistic contribution to knowledge."
- Determine whether your students are being paid by you or the mentor's organization. The institution paying the student typically has greater responsibility for the student's well-being and professional development.
- If you are sending students to another organization to participate in some type of research experience, it is important to develop a memorandum of understanding (MOU) between the two institutions. The MOU should spell out liabilities for each organization, what the students are expected to gain out of the experience, who will oversee the different aspects of the program, and how and when payments are made. Typically, your office of grants and contracts can help with this.

Paying students

There are multiple methods for paying your students for their research efforts. As we have explained, we find it highly important to pay students for the work that they do for both equity and professionalization reasons. We prefer to pay students a direct salary or hourly wage when possible as it allows them to forego other external employment and focus all of their efforts on their academic pursuits. Normally, offering employment will not affect their financial aid package. Please be sure to investigate the ins and outs of each method on your campus. The following are some of the most common ways students are paid.

Salary

At most campuses, students can receive an hourly salary for conducting research. In this case, students will need to go through the hiring process at your university and will need to report their hours. We also recommend that if you are able to hire students, you try to maximize your dollars by utilizing federal work study funds when appropriate. If you are paying students with federal grants, there will be some restrictions on whom you can hire. To support students who do not fall within federal regulations, look to state and/or private funds. This is considered income.

Research stipend

Stipends are typically paid when the work is measured by a product (such as a final research report) and not by time spent on the project. The stipend amount varies greatly between projects and institutions; it is advisable to explore what other similar programs in your area are providing students to set your stipend amount. Stipends are usually paid out at two points in time to ensure students are financially supported and work is complete. Stipends are considered income.

Fellowship

For summer research, students are often paid a fellowship, which allows them to be supported by funding as they complete a defined research project or experience. Summer fellowships generally do not affect students' financial aid if they are processed like stipends. Check with your campus to determine whether this is the case. Fellowships are considered income.

Scholarships

Scholarships are merit or need based and, strictly speaking, students should not be expected to perform tasks in order to receive a scholarship.

Other considerations and potential collaborations

It is important for your office to work closely with the financial aid office at your institution. For students who receive financial aid, any additional earnings (including scholarships) may affect their financial aid package. This is complicated and varies as different institutions interpret state and federal regulations differently. This is definitely one area where it is extremely helpful to have an ally in the financial aid office who can help you navigate the best option for different students.

Another office that may be helpful is the international center. International students have different eligibility for earnings and scholarships and it is important that the research experience does not jeopardize their visa status.

Funding research supplies

If your office has funding for research supplies, there should be a process for requesting and purchasing research supplies. Some questions to consider when establishing the process:

- Will your office purchase the supplies for students? Do you have enough staffing to be making hundreds of purchases? How will you collect the information regarding the purchases (exact model number and quantity, where to ship the items, etc.)? Will you have a deadline for making the purchases?
- Will your students be making the purchases and then be reimbursed? Can students afford to carry the cost on their credit card while waiting one to three months for the reimbursement? What process will there be to ensure that the purchases will be reimbursed (in case student purchases are over-budget or not allowable)?
- Will faculty members or departments be making the purchases? How will your office reimburse them? What are allowable purchases?
- Can researchers purchase low-value gift cards to give to survey participants? (At our institution, as long as the approved Institutional Review Board (IRB) protocol includes this, it is allowed.) Are cell phones, tablets, and laptops allowed? (At our institution, these are allowed but researchers are required to "return" the items to the university at the end of their project, unless the items have been significantly modified or have been incorporated into another piece of equipment.)

Funding student travel

Most undergraduate research offices provide some type of student travel funding. It is extremely important that you have a detailed process that is consistent with the university's travel policies.

- Determine activities that qualify for funding – presenting at conferences, attending conferences, fieldwork, visiting archives, etc.
- Ensure all liability waivers and travel authorization forms are completed ahead of time.

- Ensure students understand the budget and what is included in the reimbursement (per diem vs. reimbursing the actual cost of food, for example). At some institutions, students cannot claim the expense of poster printing for a conference as part of their travel expenses.
- Ensure students retain detailed receipts for all reimbursable charges. At our institution, the student needs to have paid for the expenses themselves to be reimbursed. If they use someone else's credit card, the university will not consider this a student-paid expense.
- If a student is traveling internationally, ensure the student works to apply for the various permissions early. They will likely need to obtain international travel insurance as well as a higher administrative approval. Risk management and the international center should be able to help with international travel.
- Some states have instituted travel bans to certain states. Stay updated on the list and have a plan for what to do if a student needs to travel to a banned state – there is usually a process to apply for exemptions.
- For students who receive travel funding from your office, will you require a short report on their experience? Ask them to fill out a post-travel survey? Or any other type of reporting or feedback regarding their travel? Be prepared to collect any data you will need to report back to your institution or your funders.

Databases and information tracking

Tracking who you serve, how you serve them, and the outcomes for those that you serve is often an afterthought. The fun part of the work is planning for the events and interacting with students. Keeping meticulous and detailed data is time consuming and not glamorous. However, it is important and can go a long way to help your office justify sustained or increased funding – and will be a requirement of most extramural funders.

- Start simple. If nothing else, keep track of students that you interact with by recording their student record number. Decide early on if you want to keep track of all students you come in contact with (office visits, workshops, paid research projects, etc.) or just those that receive money from you. Being consistent reduces a lot of work later on to clean your data.
- More advanced data keeping will separate students based on engagement level. For example, office visits might count as a low engagement level, attending a workshop may be medium engagement, and presenting at a conference could be high engagement. Again, being consistent here reduces the work later on.

- Contact your institutional research office to possibly collaborate on analyzing your data. They can probably provide you with some demographic and academic information on your service population.
- Contact your registrar's office to possibly tag students based on the list of student IDs you collected. This will make longitudinal tracking of student outcomes much simpler.

Summary: managing the ever-changing bureaucratic landscape

The difficult truth is that you will never fully get a handle on navigating the bureaucracy on your campus. Administrators leave and new administrators could interpret the same set of rules differently. Federal and state regulations change. The person you relied on in the financial aid office might retire. Be prepared to make this a continual and consistent part of what you do. Schedule regular updates to your administration. Keeping the accomplishments of student researchers top of mind for your campus will make future requests for funding easier. Express gratitude to your campus allies regularly. This will make it more likely for them to work with you when you need an exception to a rule or have an especially complicated request.

External grants, state funding, and institutional budgets all can ebb and flow. Establishing your minimal viable product (MVP) – the basic things your office absolutely needs to do in order to fulfill your mission – will help you weather the lean times. For example, your office does not need to always fund 50 students for summer research, but you must be able to provide an annual research conference for your students. Understanding your MVP will help you establish expectations and negotiate resources for your office.

Lastly, try not to let the frustrations of working through a bureaucracy obscure the joys of working with and supporting students! Bureaucracy can be seen as a hurdle but it can also be used to your office's benefit. By having to collect data and share your successes with the campus, you are also reminding yourself and your team of the important work that your office accomplishes.

VIGNETTE 9.1   Navigating institutional bureaucracy

Dr. Anne Boettcher, Assistant Dean of Research,
Embry-Riddle Aeronautical University, Prescott Campus

Every institution has their process for doing things and their priorities for what should be done. These can sometimes seem like insurmountable barriers when trying to develop or grow an undergraduate research, scholarship, and creative activity (URSCA) program. Instead, think of your institutional bureaucracy as the guide for your approach.

Start with your institution's vision, mission, and values – what parts of those can you draw on to illustrate where URSCA fits into the priorities for your campus? For example, at Embry-Riddle Aeronautical University (ERAU), the work of the Undergraduate Research Institute, Prescott campus, aligns well with the campus vision with a "focus on undergraduate education that emphasizes problem-based discovery." Where do the program goals align with your strategic plan (and if they do not align, how can you work to align or integrate into new plans)? Use the same language as your institution to help make your case. You can also use literature to demonstrate how URSCA programs help support institutional goals that center around grade point average (GPA), retention, and graduation rates. Battaglia et al. provide direct evidence that helps support the importance of research experiences.[2]

It is also important to consider how you can work with partners across campus to help support their goals and in turn demonstrate the importance of URSCA on campus. Undergraduate research is a great recruitment tool. Think about working with your admissions office, allowing your students' success to speak to the importance of research for their development and inclusion on campus. At ERAU, we couple our celebrations of undergraduate research with our campus open houses and orientation events. Similarly, share the students' stories with marketing and philanthropy. This will provide these units with the stories they need and in turn will serve to identify potential donors for your programs and projects.

As career readiness is increasingly valued, linking the benefits of undergraduate research to career readiness and working with career services to promote this on campus and with industry partners is a critical way to illustrate the importance of URSCA.[3] ERAU undergraduate research students help with career expo preparation sessions, sharing with students how their research experiences impacted their success in securing internships. Students also showcase their research during our career expo, providing a direct demonstration of their skills to company recruiters.

I should note that in every case I have shared, the first partnerships our URI made with our research librarians and communication faculty (and now our new Writing Center) have been the most important. These partners are key to the success of our students' understanding of the research process and their ability to share their stories. Our students are our best spokespeople. As noted earlier, finding ways for them to share will convince even the most resistant. Not everyone will buy in all at once; you will always be making the case, overcoming hurdles with hiring, access, and recognition for both students and faculty. Building partnerships will grow your champions across campus and provide examples when you face the next naysayer.

VIGNETTE 9.2   Building a summer research
program at a community college

Dr. Marianne Smith
Director of the Institute for Completion,
Citrus College, Retired

Background

Citrus College, a public community college and designated Hispanic-Serving Institution (HSI) in Southern California, launched the STEM Summer Research Experience (SRE) program in 2012 with resources from a US Department of Education Title III, Part F grant award. Starting small, the college supported eight students who were placed in faculty labs at a neighboring four-year university. The college provided supplies to faulty mentors and supported the student stipends.

The SRE program has grown to serve up to 60 students annually in local summer research placements and has supported student applications to other research experiences across the United States as well as in Latin America and Europe.

Building a summer research program for community college students

Student outcomes from the initial year of the program indicated additional campus students would benefit from participation. In order to expand, and in the absence of formal research laboratories on the community college campus, the college built collaborative relationships with eight institutions including multiple universities, a non-profit science laboratory, a botanic garden, a hospital research center, and a local NASA facility. Each partner agreed to accept from 1 to 12 students during the eight-week SRE period.

Each cross-sector partnership differed – some relied on the college to support the student stipends and the faculty laboratory supplies while others, happy to receive diverse students from an HSI, used their institutional funds to support stipends. In one case, an administrator from the community college collaborated with university faculty to write and secure an NSF REU grant specifically for community college students.

The terms of the relationships have been modified as extramural funding ended or began and new partnerships emerged. Citrus

College now includes funding for SRE into new STEM grant applications whether they are the lead agency or a subaward. Additionally, the college Foundation has raised funds and become a partner in supporting SRE students.

Recruitment and selection of participants

Understanding that a large percentage of early community college STEM students are apt to depart STEM or college altogether, the college primarily focuses on recruiting and selecting the students for whom the experience will be transformative and lead to retention and persistence. Applications are screened using a campus-made rubric in order to identify the target population. The college purposefully avoids the limitations of a required minimum GPA in order to attract and identify promising students who would most benefit from the opportunity.

Each applicant attends an in-person interview, allowing the selection committee to better understand the applicant's unique needs and goals. In part, the college looks for students who may not have had other extra-curricular opportunities, those who do not have access to professional role models, and those who are seeking clarity for their educational trajectory. Selected students tend to be very low-income, first-generation, and unsure how they might apply their intended degree.

In some cases, the partner institution selects students from a pool of previously screened applicants while other partners prefer the college make the final selection.

Lessons learned

Most of the selected students at the college have considerable doubts about their own ability to successfully complete SRE as they don't have role models who have had similar opportunities. As such, the college has identified a few best practices to support students in advance of, during and following, their SRE participation. In part these include:

- Connecting applicants to a system of distributed mentors who can support their needs with financial aid, course/transfer planning, mental health, etc.
- Providing a pre-experience preparation session that includes approaches to reading scientific literature and writing a literature review, creating a scientific poster, understanding lab hierarchy and strategies for communicating needs, ideas, etc.
- Leading a mid-experience poster workshop. While we recognize students will be receiving support from on-site mentors and peers,

creating a poster can be anxiety producing and the review session in a familiar environment allows students to ask questions, try on ideas, and get feedback.

- Sending students regular prompts via email giving them an avenue to voice concerns and share successes. In reviewing prompts, we can identify where we may need to speak with the site coordinator to resolve potential conflict.
- Holding an on-campus fall symposium that all participants are required to attend. This not only helps them solidify their own learning but is an important recruitment tool for future cohorts and it has provided opportunities for faculty to reimagine the capacity of community college students' potential.

Notes

1 UROC website – see https://csumb.edu/uroc/getting-started/#:~:text= Internships%20vs.%20 undergraduate%20research%3A%20 What%27s%20 the%20 difference%3F
2 Battaglia, S.J., et al. "Institution-Wide Analysis of Academic Outcomes Associated with Participation in UGR: Comparison of Different Research Modalities at a Hispanic-Serving Institution." *Scholarship and Practice of Undergraduate Research, the Journal of the Council on Undergraduate Research*, vol. 5 no. 3, 2022, 8–24, https://doi.org/10.18833/spur/5/3/9
3 Mekolichick, J. Position Paper: *Recognizing Undergraduate Research, Scholarship, & Creative Inquiry as a Career-Readiness Tool*. Council on Undergraduate Research, 2023, www.cur.org/impact/position_statement_career_readiness__ur/

References

Banks, J.E., et al. "Alliance for Change: Broadening Participation in Undergraduate Research at California State University." *Scholarship and Practice of Undergraduate Research (SPUR)*, vol. 1 no. 4, 2018, 5–11.
Battaglia, S.J., et al. "Institution-Wide Analysis of Academic Outcomes Associated with Participation in UGR: Comparison of Different Research Modalities at a Hispanic-Serving Institution." *Scholarship and Practice of Undergraduate Research, the Journal of the Council on Undergraduate Research*, vol. 5 no. 3, 2022, 8–24, https://doi.org/10.18833/spur/5/3/9
Mekolichick, J. Position Paper: *Recognizing Undergraduate Research, Scholarship, & Creative Inquiry as a Career-Readiness Tool*. Council on Undergraduate Research, 2023, www.cur.org/impact/position_statement_career_readiness__ur/

10 Getting the word out to students

Yet another of the big challenges facing any undergraduate research office – new or established – is connecting with the students your program is designed to serve. Students move through our campuses in a multitude of ways. While some will frequent official or unofficial student gathering places where they are likely to see a nicely designed flyer, others dip in and out of campus for their classes, never entering the café or student lounge. Electronic outreach is similarly hit or miss. Some students will read an email solicitation, but many others will not. There will always be a small number of students who come to campus looking for a way to engage in undergraduate research. These students will find you because they know what they are looking for. But how do you ensure that all the other students know your office exists, understand what it has to offer them, and feel comfortable enough with your messaging to take that first step through your door and ask the question "how can I be part of this"?

Determining the right kind of outreach: messaging

There is no one-size-fits-all approach to connecting with students, so understanding your target audience is the first step in determining your outreach approach. Is your office doing outreach to a school or program with which you hope to build a pipeline? Do you want to reach first year students (freshman or transfers), or are you looking for students with sophomore or junior standing? Are you looking to engage students from a particular department or program, or from across your entire campus? Are you looking for students who are already participating in other leadership activities and high-impact practices, or are you focused on reaching out to students who have not had these opportunities prior to coming to college? Most of our programs have a specific emphasis on first-generation, low-income, and/or underrepresented student groups, because we know that increasing a student's understanding of undergraduate research is a key way to help them achieve their long-term academic and/or professional goals, so while

DOI: 10.4324/9781003154952-10

we create broadly inclusive messaging, we tend to focus on the needs of those students.

Ultimately, you should do the same kinds of assessment of your campus, students, and programmatic goals that we have recommended in prior chapters, when determining the kinds of marketing and outreach messages you want to produce. While it is important to tailor your approach, we can offer a couple of examples that we have used to get your creative juices flowing.

Demystifying undergraduate research

For many students, the meaning of the term "undergraduate research" is a mystery, especially if they have chosen to attend a community college, or a primarily undergraduate institution (PUI). They may have a general sense of what it is but might also feel that it is not for them or that they are not prepared to participate, or are not the "right kind of student."[1] Because of this, finding ways to demystify and humanize undergraduate research is really important.

At CSU Monterey Bay, the UROC program developed an ongoing campaign called *This is What A Researcher Looks Like* (see Figure 10.1 on the following page), that began with an idea for a t-shirt. After passing the shirts out to our students to wear around campus, we began to feature a series of researcher profiles on our social media (Facebook and Instagram) with the same tagline. Our goal was to reach more students with the message that students who look like you, share your interests or background, and whom you might even know – are doing research. In short, that this is something they could do too.

In addition to humanizing undergraduate research, scholarship, and creative activity (URSCA), the series was a way for our office to celebrate the work of our students more publicly, outside of the formality of end-of-year celebrations and award ceremonies. A final part of this campaign took place within our introductory workshops where students were given large sheets of butcher paper and asked to draw their image of a "researcher." Not surprisingly, many drew the stereotypical stick figure in a lab coat. UROC staff work with them to analyze their presumptions and expand their images to the point that they see themselves, and their own unique academic interests, emerge on paper.

The benefits of undergraduate research

As we have discussed in prior chapters, across the country, there are lower rates of participation in undergraduate research for students who are BIPOC, first-generation, low-income, transfers, adult learners, and Pell-eligible. Despite hearing about URSCA in a variety of ways, students who

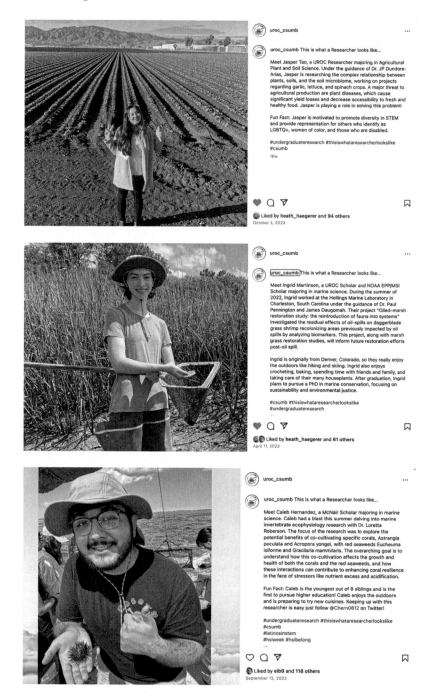

Figure 10.1 Sample social media posts from CSU Monterey Bay's *This is What a Researcher Looks Like* campaign.

benefit the most from participation may not understand the benefits of the practice, or feel like they can overcome the barriers they perceive to their participation.[2] Because of this, it is important to work to create positive patterns of inclusivity by working with other programs on campus that may serve these students (TRIO, Educational Opportunity Program (EOP), transfer student centers, affinity or identity-based centers, etc.), as well as offer clear messaging to students about the ways they will be supported if they take the risk and try something new (peer groups, writing support, tutoring, advising, etc.). Some of the most compelling ways we have found to describe the benefits of undergraduate research to students include messages that stress that URSCA is for you because it will help you:

- explore new academic interests.
- improve your oral and written communication skills.
- develop your self-confidence.
- raise your grade point average (GPA).
- develop new and useful skills.
- participate in the creation of new knowledge.
- prepare you for graduate school and the workforce.
- gain expertise that will help you change the world someday.

Getting your message out

As you may have guessed, we don't have a magic formula for marketing your program or getting the word out. What we do know is that you will need to work to reach students in multiple ways. Our experience has taught us two things: the first is that students most often find their way to our programs because they know someone else who participated and had a positive experience, or because they heard a student or students give a presentation about their undergraduate research experience. Our takeaway? Peer messaging is extremely important. Second, if you are going to utilize online communication or social media to reach your students, you need to be flexible with your messaging, and be ready to consistently try new approaches. In other words, be aware of the generational divides that separate your online activity from your students', which are far more likely to be constantly changing. We recommend you consider hiring a student to advise you or manage that aspect of your outreach; they will know where their peers are gathering online and what kind of message they are likely to respond to. Across our offices, we deploy most, if not all, of the following:

Electronic outreach:

- email – to professors, department chairs, undergraduate advisors, and other staff is an effective way to make sure your programs get announced in class. Seventy percent students report that they first heard about undergraduate research from a professor.[3]

- Social media posts and social media takeovers are more effective for reaching students directly and drawing new audiences to your program. If you are going to utilize social media though, you need to have a plan. What sorts of things will you post? How often will you post? Who will oversee creating the right "brand" for your office or program – one that will both speak to students, and to the other audiences that are sure to find you: staff, faculty, administration, donors, etc.? A little bit of time spent creating a media plan before launching right into social media will go a long way.

- Finally, ensuring program descriptions and application deadlines are cross-listed in departmental e-communications and newsletters is important, as students are more likely to read these than other forms of campus communication.

Posters and flyers

We still make (and recommend) flyers for many of our programs, especially those with application deadlines, and for the in-person undergraduate research events we host. The more that students see your logo and office name around campus, the more likely they are to come to an event, workshop, or research presentation. While you will want to create simple, yet eye-catching print media, be sure that your color scheme, logo, and overall "look" is consistent across everything you produce and that it matches your electronic outreach. If you don't feel that you have the design skills necessary, we recommend hiring a student to help with your design – take advantage of the expertise on your campus! – or try utilizing the free templates that are available through platforms like Piktochart, Creately, or even those templates available as part of your word processing program.[4] As much as we hate to say it, design, branding, and brand recognition are important.

Personalized outreach: ambassadors and peers

The single most powerful tool you have when it comes to recruiting for your programs is the student you are already serving. While most students first *hear* about undergraduate research from a professor, the majority of those who take the next step and come into an office, join a workshop, or apply to a program, will do so because they have a friend who is already participating, or because they spoke to another student who had a good experience. Because of this, we have found that student ambassadors are the best way to get the word out to other students – instead of going into classes yourself to give a recruiting presentation, send your students! Their messages about what they have learned and how much they love research will be far more powerful than anything you could say yourself.

Workshops

There is a standard repertoire of workshops that most offices of undergraduate research, scholarship, and creative activity offer as part of their service to campus, many of which can also serve as recruitment tools. These often include:

- Demystifying research.
- Getting involved in undergraduate research at [your campus].
- How to write a research proposal.
- Finding a summer research experience.
- Academic resume and CV writing.
- Poster design and presentation.

You can find PowerPoints for a number of these offerings on our websites, as well as the websites of undergraduate research offices around the country. We encourage you to use our templates if you are just starting out and refine your messaging to speak to the specific needs of your students.[5]

Undergraduate research week

The Council on Undergraduate Research (CUR) notes:

> On November 16, 2010, the U.S. House of Representatives declared the week of April 11, 2011, as "Undergraduate Research Week." Since that time, CUR has designated a week in April each year as "Undergraduate Research Week" a national celebration in which CUR showcases what other campuses are doing to celebrate UR[SCA], congratulate students on their research, and thank those faculty and mentors who have helped guide the way for UR.[6]

We have found that participation in undergraduate research week is an excellent way to demonstrate your campus' commitment to undergraduate research as well as to showcase the work your students are doing. Hosting a variety of events allows you to utilize the week as a recruiting tool for new students as well. Our programs have done the following as part of our annual celebrations:

- Student research talks – offered at regular times throughout the week.
- Information sessions introducing students to our office and a variety of ways to engage in URSCA, including student-led sessions featuring diverse research paths.
- Student/faculty panels where they discuss their own work and the path that led them to their current positions.
- Coffee with a researcher – a hosted coffee and goodie hour.
- College and departmental open houses – regular times throughout the week when students can drop by and visit labs, studios, research and creative spaces and ask questions, or even participate in mini research experiences.
- Research symposium – a big, day-long event featuring student talks, poster presentations, performances, and other student research, scholarship, and creative presentations.

Finally, to encourage students to participate in multiple events throughout the week, we developed a "passport" that students can have stamped at each event, with prizes offered for attending multiple events or completing the entire passport.

Low-stakes and short-term research opportunities

Many URSCA offices have found that offering opportunities to try undergraduate research, scholarly or creative activities provides students who are unsure about participating with a way to give it a try and figure out if it is right for them. The short-term, low-stakes engagements we have developed were specifically designed to address barriers to participation that students had brought up in focus groups and consultations. In response to these concerns, and building upon the relationships, resources, and faculty expertise we had on our campuses, we developed the following:

- Mini research engagements – we have asked faculty to come up with a directed, hands-on research engagement that can be completed in just a few hours as part of our undergraduate research week activities.
- Research Rookies program – drawing our inspiration from presentations we heard from colleagues at the CUR annual conference, we developed our own Research Rookies program. Geared toward first-year or transfer students, ours is a self-paced, online program where students complete nine activities ranging from reading a research article,

to participating in a citizen science project, to speaking with one of our current undergraduate research scholars.[7]

- Spring break research intensives – we developed a variable unit, special topics course taught over spring break which lets students immerse themselves in location-based, hands-on research in topics such as small mammal ecology, or gull foraging ecology.[8]
- For students in our Louis Stokes Alliance for Minority Participation (LSAMP) program, we developed a fully funded Costa Rica Research Training Expedition, a beginning research experience in which students learn the foundations of inquiry-based research, including experimental design, research methods, and analysis while exploring the spectacular ecosystems of Costa Rica.[9]

Despite our best efforts to provide several points of entry to participation in URSCA, we know that barriers still exist, which is why we recommend that campuses work to develop Course-based Research Experiences (CUREs) across the disciplines. We discuss CUREs at length in Chapter 12.

Connecting students to research opportunities

Most offices of undergraduate research, scholarship, and creative activity will not have the staff to individually match students with the right campus mentor or organized research program. Because of this, we see that many offices expect students to apply to their programs with a mentor and research project already in place. We ourselves offer some programs like these for students who have had a chance to familiarize themselves with campus, their research interests, potential mentors, etc. However, not all students will come to you with these resources in place. There are some great tools out there that you can use to help students connect to their interests, as well as help mentors connect with new students. These are useful for both large campuses, where students may need help navigating the wealth of opportunities, as well as small, where students may need to be directed to opportunities off campus, or at partner institutions.[10]

At CSU Monterey Bay, we decided to utilize a paid service called Student Opportunities Center (SOC), which allows students to find open research opportunities, including virtual opportunities, via a large searchable national database. We liked this particular service because it gathered information from across multiple platforms into one easy to use database so our students could search for year-round online opportunities, and summer research experiences across the nation. It also allowed us to customize the information to include our own campus opportunities, indicating their availability to only our students.[11] Other similar platforms are available, and we encourage you to do your research to determine if they are appropriate for your campus needs. Students can also be pointed toward the CUR website which has an entire section dedicated to student resources, including internship and research opportunities.[12]

The importance of presenting next steps/what's next

We want to end this chapter with just a few words about the importance of guidance for students at this stage. It will be really exciting to see students begin to engage with your programs – there is nothing more fulfilling than a packed room for a workshop, or a happy group of students undertaking an undergraduate research week activity. But you want to make sure that your engagement with them doesn't end there. With every piece of outreach you do, try to end with a roadmap of next steps so that the student leaves both excited and knowing where to go next. If we offer a workshop, for example, we have students sign in so we can follow up with an email with appropriate information. If the workshop was an introduction to one of our programs, this would mean following up with a summary of the key points of the workshop, the requirements for the program and its application deadline, a link to our application forms, and the contact information for someone in our office they can speak with if they want to. When our student ambassadors make a presentation in a classroom, we send them with goodies and swag (we like the fun, tri-colored pens, customized with our logo), as well as bookmark-sized handouts complete with basic programmatic and contact information. We also have them ask the class to connect with our social media right then and there – take a picture and tag or mention us! All of these methods help get us onto students' radar and help us keep in touch so that we can continue to provide them with the information they need to take the next steps in their undergraduate research journeys.

Notes

1 Once students walk in our door, we do a lot of work to help them understand the imposter phenomenon, and while our recruiting messaging may not directly speak about it, we design our process to help combat its effects.
2 Haeger, H., et al. "Creating More Inclusive Research Environments for Undergraduates." *Journal of the Scholarship of Teaching and Learning*, vol. 21 no. 1, 2021, https://doi.org/10.14434/josotl.v21i1.30101
3 Haeger et al.
4 https://piktochart.com/ or https://creately.com/
5 CSU Monterey Bay UROC office presentations can be found here: https://csumb.edu/uroc/resources/. Cal Poly Pomona OUR office presentations can be found here: www.cpp.edu/our-cpp/events-workshops/workshops.shtml

6 www.cur.org/what/events/urw/
7 You can learn more about CSUMB's Research Rookies program here: https://csumb.edu/uroc/research-rookies-program/. You can also explore programs with similar aims at UCLA www.aap.ucla.edu/programs/research-rookies/; and Highpoint University www.highpoint.edu/urcw/research-rookies/
8 https://csumb.edu/uroc/spring-intensive-courses/
9 https://csumb.edu/uroc/costa-rica-expedition/
10 In Chapter 6, we discuss connecting students to research opportunities both on and off campus in greater detail.
11 See https://csumb.edu/uroc/open-research-opportunitiess/
12 See www.cur.org/engage/undergraduate/research/

Reference

Haeger, H., et al. "Creating More Inclusive Research Environments for Undergraduates." *Journal of the Scholarship of Teaching and Learning*, vol. 21 no. 1, 2021.

11 Assessment and educational research

Assessment and program evaluation are crucial in the development of a centralized undergraduate research, scholarship, and creative activity (URSCA) office, and in sustaining it. When looking to start an URSCA center, taking a temperature of where your campus is can also help make the case for where it can be with a more centralized system. Once a center is established, formative evaluation can help you to continuously improve, and summative assessment is essential in communicating the impact of URSCA to internal audiences (e.g., campus leadership, faculty, staff, and students) as well as external funding sources or policymakers (e.g., grant funding agencies and state officials). This chapter will help you develop an assessment plan and provide concrete strategies and resources for implementing it. This chapter features resources developed for the Council on Undergraduate Research (CUR) by Dr. Haeger and can be found on the CUR Assessment website for more information.

The first step is the hardest

Before you begin your assessment planning, you should address the difficult but essential step of tracking participation in URSCA activities. Whether you have a distributed or centralized model on your campus, this can be a challenge, but setting up consistent and reliable tracking systems is the foundation of all future assessment projects. If you don't know who is doing research or scholarship, how can you assess it?

The first step in assessment is defining what you are counting as undergraduate research and creativity activity on your campus *and* consistently tracking participation.[1] That being said, tracking some participation is better than tracking nothing. It is nearly impossible to create a flawless tracking system, so start where you are and track what you can. Here are some areas to explore when thinking about tracking participation:

1. Where and how are students participating in URSCA on your campus? For example, if your campus has several ways to participate in research

DOI: 10.4324/9781003154952-11

(e.g., summer programs, independent study options, research labs) can you collect lists of students from those groups?

2. Are there places where URSCA participants come together? If there are research events on campus, can you collect lists of students presenting research or scholarly activity at those events?

3. Is there an existing source of data? If your institution already collects survey data on student engagement (e.g., National Survey of Student Engagement), they may already have questions on those surveys about participation in URSCA.

4. How else can I connect to URSCA participants? Here is the time to get creative. Is there an incentive you can offer that would encourage students to report their participation? Could you offer a research award, or mentor recognition that would encourage students or faculty to report their research? Can students receive a certificate of URSCA completion from your office, can you publish a list of URSCA projects that students would want to be on . . . ? Finding a way to encourage students to report their URSCA participation to you needs to be beneficial to your students or faculty.

5. Two offices that might be of assistance are the institutional research office, that tracks enrollment, student FTE credit hours, etc., and the office of sponsored programs. For example, if a large proportion of faculty research grants were being used to pay undergraduates to work in research labs, are these students being counted anywhere? This may be a large number of undergraduate researchers that could be tracked through a sponsored programs office.

Once you have decided how you define URSCA and how you will find participants to track, you'll need to decide what pieces of data you want to collect. Thinking about what you need to know and what you might assess, consider other items to track in addition to participation.

- Who does research? What is the demographic and academic background of the students and faculty?
- How much or for how long? Do you need to know the number of hours, weeks, terms, and/or years that students participated?
- With what intensity or rigor? Are there different types of research experiences on campus that you need to capture (e.g., short research module in a course vs. an entirely research-focused CURE, or mentored vs. course-based research, summer vs. academic term)?
- Is there funding or credit associated with participation, from whom?
- What is the product or outcome? Are there additional artifacts you would want to collect (e.g., research abstracts, conference presentation citations, student reflections during the research process, lab notes)?

Thinking about what to collect in the early stages of your assessment can save you a lot of time in the future and create a strong foundation for your future assessment.

Here is one example of how we use multiple datapoints to demonstrate the research happening at CSUMB. These graphics are used to communicate to our own campus some of the ways students engage with research

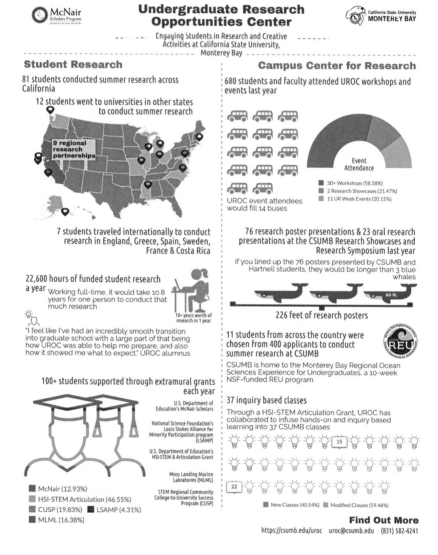

Figure 11.1 Infographic using multiple datapoints to illustrate.

and scholarly activity. The same data is also used to report on grant objectives and more traditional reporting venues.

Creating a plan

You've started tracking participation in research, now what? The next step is to think about the why, what, when, and how of your assessment and create a plan of action.

Why are you assessing URSCA?

Start with the root of why you are assessing URSCA as this will be your guidepost. Are you assessing for specific reporting purposes, to improve support for students, to secure funding for your programs, to disseminate findings in presentations or publications? Often the answer to this question involves multiple whys, but think about the audience for each one separately. The type of data and analysis your campus president will want to see may be very different than the type of findings you would present in a journal article; your campus president might want a one-page summary of project activities and a summary of outcomes, but a journal reviewer might want a much more nuanced and detailed analysis and presentation of findings. Similarly, if you are primarily assessing for program improvement, a less formal and structured means for students and faculty to provide feedback might be sufficient; whereas, if you are reporting assessment results in an annual report for a grant, you may need a more structured and systematic approach.

What are you assessing?

This aspect focuses on what you measure and what outcomes you are looking for. I suggest having a group conversation or doing a free write to answer the following question: if you had a magic wand, what outcome would you want to see for your students, faculty, and/or campus? What do you value? What do you hope students get out of their research experience? What do you think changes as a result of your program for students, faculty, the campus, the community? These questions will help you generate potential areas of assessment, but don't get bogged down in the practicability of measuring these goals, that will come next. Give yourself or your team time to dream big about what outcomes are meaningful for your URSCA program, then you can move onto what is measurable. In thinking about what is measurable, think about what data you or your campus already collects. Think broadly: research products (posters, abstract, presentations), institutional data on grades and retention, previously collected surveys, student reflections, feedback forms. As we like to remind folks, anything can be data. For example, at CSUMB, we asked students to keep a blog during their summer URSCA experience and analyzed the blogs for identification with their discipline and future goals.

When you've generated a list of outcomes that are meaningful on your campus and data you already have access to, you can look for points of alignment. Is there any data already being collected on your campus that can provide evidence as to whether those meaningful outcomes are happening for your students or faculty? Are there new sources of data you need to start collecting?

Assessment tips by data type

Check for previously established instruments (e.g., look for concept inventories for discipline-specific knowledge and literature in psychology, education, and social sciences for measures of learning and development). If you do not find a survey instrument that meets your needs, consider the following when creating your own survey:

- Only ask for what you'll use, in order to keep surveys short.
- Ask about behavior or content knowledge when possible.
- Utilize self-reported learning when appropriate.[2] Self-reported learning includes survey or interview questions where you ask students how much they have learned, gained, developed in an area (e.g., to what extent did your summer research contribute to your understanding of the research process) or where students rate their own abilities in a pre- or post-test (e.g., please rate your ability to work on a team with other researchers). This type of data is strongly tied to satisfaction and limited by the students' ability to know what they don't know. For example, students often rate themselves higher on pre-tests and lower on tests after research experiences, once they have seen how much they have to learn. However, this data can be useful when used in the following ways:
- Comparisons between treatments (e.g., students who did undergraduate research compared to those who didn't).
- Relationships between items (e.g., the relationship between reporting feeling supported by a faculty mentor and self-reported learning).
- When compared to another measure to increase validity (e.g., is self-reported learning related to increases in grade point average (GPA), retention, graduation rates, or faculty evaluation of learning).

In addition to survey data, you may want to collect qualitative data including interviews, focus groups, student reflections, writing samples, or student products like research papers or posters. To analyze this data, you can use rubrics or create a coding structure.[3]

When are you assessing which aspects of your program?

It is important that you choose what research to do when. A common pitfall in creating an assessment plan is to be so overwhelmed with the possibilities, that it feels impossible to pick a direction and move. One way to move through this is to think of your assessment in stages. Pick something you can assess now by using data you have or can easily get access to, then plan ahead for data collection for the future. Consider what resources you have, what your time frame is, what the purpose and the *audience* of the assessment is, and how you will communicate your findings when creating your research plan.

How will you complete this assessment?

This can encompass both the resources you will need to complete this assessment and the question of who will do what. In thinking about how you will conduct this assessment, remember the power of collaboration and aligned interests. Looking across your own campus can be a great place to start. Many universities have faculty in the fields of education and the social sciences who might be interested in working with you on URSCA-related research. Beyond your institution, what connections do you have? This can be an avenue to find faculty interested in collaborating on URSCA-related research. There are also URSCA-related surveys conducted through other universities that may be helpful to you.[4]

The question of *how* should also be answered in consideration with the *why*, *what*, and *when* of your assessment plan. You will have to balance the scope of your assessment plan within the resources you have available to you. Often, starting small with the resources you have now can help you gather some preliminary data which can then help you advocate for additional resources in terms of funding or staff time on campus.

Sample assessment plan

To see how these principles can be enacted, we will show you the why, what, when, and how for the Undergraduate Research Opportunities Center (UROC) at CSUMB assessment plan.

Why?

The overarching goals of our assessment are to maximize student development through URSCA and provide models of effective practices to other institutions. To assess student development, we examine how curricular changes, student support services, writing interventions, type and quality of mentoring, and experiences in research impact students' self-efficacy, identity, academic achievement and aspirations, and leadership. We are also exploring how distributed research placements, cohort development, mentor training, community involvement, collaboration between institutions, and scaffolding levels of programmatic interventions can engage traditionally underrepresented students and foster rigorous research experiences for students from community colleges, primarily undergraduate institutions, and minority-serving institutions.

The audience for our assessment includes internal audiences (our own staff and faculty mentors in order to improve our own practices), campus leadership, community donors, and grant administrators. Additionally, we have structured our assessment to assess models of effective practices for conference presentation and journal publications.

What?

To meet our assessment goals, we gather the following types of data:

- Pre- and post-mentored research surveys.
- Institutional data (URSCA participants and non-participant peers).
- Course-based Research Experience surveys.
- Faculty assessment of their research mentee.
- Senior exit interviews.
- Focus groups (with participants and non-participants).
- Written reflection and blog posts.
- Research products (papers, posters, presentations).
- Alumni survey and interviews.

When and how?

This may look overwhelming, but the amount of data we collect started from institutional data collected through the university and a pre- and post-research test ten years ago. As we have grown the office and added more staff (including a staff position dedicated to program assessment and educational research), we have been able to scale-up our assessment too. Our initial assessment plan started with deciding on pre- and post-surveys which we have continued to collect yearly for the past ten years. We have slowly added new sources of data, some of which we collect annually (i.e., surveys, interviews, focus groups, reflections), and some that we collect periodically on staggered years (i.e., alumni survey and interviews, faculty evaluations).

Ready set assess

To start creating your own assessment plan, we invite you to work through your own why, what, when, and how, using the following worksheet.

Once you have worked through the answers to these questions, it is time to take action.

1. Outline the learning outcomes, skills, or benefits you hope your students are getting out of their research experience.[5]
2. Which of these can you measure with data you already have? Create a question you can answer now based on that.
3. Which outcomes can you find ways to measure in the future? Create longer-term questions for those.
4. Take the first step; set up a plan for who is doing what when to start gathering data and moving your assessment forward!

A common first step is to find out if your research and assessment qualifies as human subjects research or a quality improvement activity.[6] Educational assessment of undergraduate research often falls under the category of quality improvement activities and can be done within the limits of typical education activities. This type of assessment may then be exempt

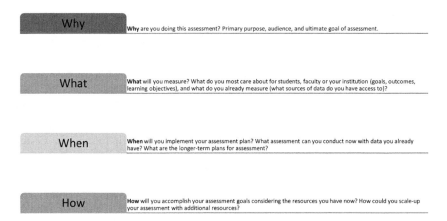

Figure 11.2 Create your own assessment plan.

from Institutional Review Board (IRB) requirements. Check with your IRB about qualifying for exemption. Here are some tips that generally help:

- If you don't need it, don't collect personal identifiers. If you are not going to match this survey, interview, or focus group to other sources of data in the future, do not collect student names or identifiers so there is no risk of identification.
- Utilize previously established educational practices. If your intervention is something new that has never been tested before, you will need IRB oversight. If you are testing the implementation of something that has been previously tested like active learning, hands-on projects, or project-based learning, your research is more likely to be exempt.
- Utilize data from traditional educational activities or student products (e.g., research papers or course exams).
- Research that is a case study or that is primarily to inform quality improvement activities for your program or university is more likely to be exempt.

Even if you believe your research will be exempt, check to see if you need IRB approval before you conduct your assessment. Consult with your IRB to determine if your assessment falls under Human Subject Protection or if it is considered a "quality improvement activity." Even if you do not need IRB approval, follow ethical research practices and remember that any data that contains information about students is also protected by Family Educational Rights and Privacy Act (FERPA).[7]

Notes

1 See the Council on Undergraduate Research (CUR). "Quarterly Special Issue on Assessment of Undergraduate Research." Spring, vol. 35 no. 3, 2015 for additional assessment strategies.
2 See: Pike, G. "Using College Students' Self-Reported Learning Outcomes in Scholarly Research." *New Directions for Institutional Research*, no. 150, 2011, 41–58.
3 Resources on rubrics: AAC&U Value Rubrics: www.aacu.org/value-rubrics and www.aacu.org/meetings/assessment-that-empowers
4 The Council on Undergraduate Research (CUR) Assessment Toolkit lists a number of commonly used URSCA survey instruments. "Assessment Tools – The Council on Undergraduate Research." 2023, www.cur.org/resources-publications/mentor-resources/assessment-tools/
5 See a review of questions that have been reviewed in literature on undergraduate research (UR) in CUR quarterly: Crowe and Brakke (2008). Assessing the Impact of Undergraduate Research Experiences on Students: An Overview of Current Literature: www.cur.org/assets/1/7/summer08CroweBrakke1.PDF

6 See the revised common rule for references on determining if your research and assessment qualifies as needing Human Subjects protection: www.hhs.gov/ohrp/ education-and-outreach/revised-common-rule/revised-common-rule-q-and-a/ index.html and you should always consult with the Institutional Review Board at your institution.

7 FERPA resources: https://www2.ed.gov/policy/gen/guid/fpco/ferpa/students.html

References

American Association of Colleges & Universities. *VALUE Rubrics*. American Association of Colleges & Universities, 2024, www.aacu.org/initiatives/ value-initiative/value-rubrics

Crowe, M., and D. Brakke. "Assessing the Impact of Undergraduate Research Experiences on Students: An Overview of Current Literature." *CUR Quarterly*, vol. 28 no. 4, 2008, 43–50.

Office for Human Research Protections. "Revised Common Rule Q&As. HHS. gov." 2022, www.hhs.gov/ohrp/education-and-outreach/revised-common-rule/ revised-common-rule-q-and-a/index.html

Pike, G.R. "Using College Students' Self-Reported Learning Outcomes in Scholarly Research." *New Directions for Institutional Research*, vol. 2011 no. 150, 2011, 41–58, https://doi.org/10.1002/ir.388

The Council on Undergraduate Research. "Assessment Tools – The Council on Undergraduate Research." 2023, www.cur.org/resources-publications/ mentor-resources/assessment-tools/

US Department of Education (ED). "Family Educational Rights and Privacy Act (FERPA)." 2021, https://www2.ed.gov/policy/gen/guid/fpco/ferpa/index.html

12 Scaling up access and reducing barriers to undergraduate research: Course-based Undergraduate Research Experiences and faculty mentor development

Although there are numerous benefits to undergraduate research for students who are minoritized in educational settings (students of color, first-generation college students, students from lower-income families, or transfer students),[1] research indicates that they are less likely to participate or stay in mentored research experiences[2] than traditionally privileged students. A recent mixed-methods study of an undergraduate research program at one of our campuses (led by Dr. Heather Haeger at California State University, Monterey Bay), identified a number of barriers to participation in research for underrepresented students.[3] This chapter will describe these findings and provide examples of interventions that have been developed to increase access to research, diversify research participation, and create more inclusive research environments.

While increasing access to research is a fundamental step toward increasing equity in high-impact practices, it is equally important to ensure that research environments are inclusive spaces for students. Proven strategies to increase inclusivity include highlighting the contributions of scholars from diverse backgrounds[4] and creating structures to ensure both positive peer support and inclusive faculty mentoring in research.[5] In this chapter, we will present two activities we designed to create more inclusive research environments: *Sticky Situations* and *The Game of Undergraduate Research*. *Sticky Situations*, a game where students work through difficult scenarios using a framework for complex decision-making, has teams of students discuss how they would solve problems or respond to microaggressions in research experiences. Based on *The Game of Life*, *The Game of Undergraduate Research* takes the findings of research on barriers to participation and has faculty work through those barriers and reflect on how their practices could be more inclusive.

Framework for inclusive research environments

In our 2021 work, we conducted a mixed-methods study in order to explore URSCA representation and URSCA inclusivity for marginalized

DOI: 10.4324/9781003154952-12

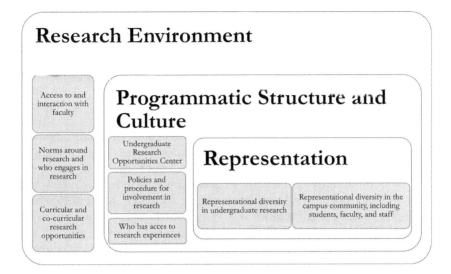

Figure 12.1 **Conceptual model of inclusivity.** Intersectional levels of inclusivity starting with representation, then programmatic structure and culture, both within the larger campus research environment.

students at California State University (CSU) Monterey Bay, a diverse predominantly undergraduate institution. The findings and interventions described in this chapter are organized within a conceptual framework for inclusive research environments.

We conceptualize inclusivity as a continuum instead of a dichotomous "inclusive" or "exclusive" environment, while recognizing that experiences of inclusivity are not monolithic. An environment which is inclusive and supportive for some students may be exclusive for others. Additionally, mesosystems within universities such as policies, programs, and structures interact to shape students' social interactions and sense of belonging.[6] The research informing this chapter examines how inclusive the environment is and to whom it is inclusive through an interactional model of social and environmental factors adapted from BrckaLorenz, Haeger, and Priddie's model for inclusive education environments.[7] In this model, we examine how university culture, structures, policies, and programs intersect and interact in order to create more inclusive or exclusive environments within the nested levels of representation, program structure and culture, and research environments. Strategies for creating more inclusive research experiences for students are presented within these nested concepts.

Representation

Though we found that representational diversity was achieved at California State University, Monterey Bay (CSUMB), research at other universities has demonstrated that most undergraduate research programs do not have representational diversity.[8] Issues of underrepresentation are a significant problem in undergraduate research, scholarship, and creative activity (URSCA) with significantly fewer students of color, first-generation, low-income, and transfer students participating in undergraduate research, even at minority-serving institutions.[9] The higher level of representation at CSUMB was likely due to outreach efforts and the financial support provided by grant initiatives aimed at increasing diversity in research. CSUMB used two Department of Education grants (the Ronald E. McNair Postbaccalaureate Achievement Program and a Department of Education Hispanic Serving Institution STEM and Articulation grant) to provide funding for undergraduate researchers, fund outreach to traditionally underrepresented populations, and fund academic positions that support students in finding research placements and facilitate professional development. These programs, along with a campus commitment to diversity, have worked to break patterns of unequal participation in research in terms of race and class.[10] Despite the success of these efforts, we found that transfer students were still less likely to engage in research, and a significant population of the students who believed that research would benefit them in their education and career goals were not able to participate. These findings point to the need for the creation of more opportunities and stronger outreach to lower-division, community college, and recent transfer students.

Representation intervention: the community college apprentice research experience

The community college apprenticeship research experience (CCARE) program was created at CSUMB in 2018 in order to provide an opportunity for community college students to connect with the campus community and conduct research with university faculty before deciding to transfer. Through outreach and collaboration with local and statewide community colleges, we aimed to recruit both incoming transfer students and students who intended to transfer to any four-year college. Once selected, students participated in a 9–10-week research experience were connected with appropriate university resources and were highly encouraged to live with their cohort of CCARE students on campus. The summer concluded with a summer research symposium where all undergraduate researchers presented their findings. In 2019, this symposium included 25 oral presentations and over 80 posters from students conducting research at the university and with regional research partners.

Representation intervention: Course-based Undergraduate Research
Experiences

Course-based Undergraduate Research Experiences (CUREs) are often touted as a way to increase opportunities for students to engage in research.[11] The creation of CUREs targeting recent transfer students and lower-division students can provide earlier contact with tenure-track faculty, as well as an introductory research experience for more students. The volume *Course-based Undergraduate Research Educational Equity and High-Impact Practice* outlines several initiatives that target students in lower division courses.[12] For example, faculty at North Seattle College and Central Washington University have collaborated to develop an Interdisciplinary Investigation (IDI)-Lab for first-year community college students with an emphasis on investigative skills. In their chapter titled "A High-throughput model for CUREs for the first two years of Chemistry and Biology," the authors discuss the creation of IDI-Lab and report student self-assessed gains (increased confidence in science communication) as determined via the CURE survey.[13]

At CSUMB, we have created a CURE Faculty Fellows program in order to support faculty to develop courses that engage students in authentic research experiences. This program is currently in its third year and is funded by the Provost and a supplement to our US Department of Education Hispanic-Serving Institution STEM and Articulation Grant. Like the creators of IDI-Lab, our goal is to engage students in collaborative, authentic research experiences and to encourage the integration of CUREs across departments. In order to support faculty in developing Course-based Research Experiences, the CURE Faculty Fellows program provides pay for up to 72 hours of work (based on summer salary rate). During this funded time, faculty work together in a community of practice to develop new courses or redesign existing courses to include research experiences.

In addition to providing time for course development, campuses should consider how else they can incentivize the inclusion of research in courses, including how it is documented and evaluated in tenure and promotion consideration, and how they are messaging to students. Recent research demonstrated that telling students explicitly that they are engaging in research and that the naming of courses as CUREs shapes the learning outcomes of the class.[14] They found that only students in courses specifically identified as CUREs increased in their self-identification as researchers when compared to students in a control group who took the same course but without the CURE label. Making course-based research opportunities visible and available to students can increase access for students traditionally excluded from research experiences.

Program structure and culture

Looking beyond representation, we found a number of other barriers to full inclusion in research. At the programmatic level, navigating academic structures, like applying for funding through a campus program, or finding a research placement with faculty on campus, were significant barriers to many students. Students requested a centralized way to learn about research happening on campus instead of having to email individual faculty or only having access to faculty that they currently had classes with. Students also wanted explicit and clear information about the availability of funding for research and the application process. Furthermore, even though the university offers a number of funded opportunities, many students were unaware of them. Students also felt that the undergraduate research office, and research in general, were intimidating, exclusive spaces.

Program structure and culture intervention: scholar spotlights

At CSUMB, our office collaborated with Dr. Corin Slown (faculty, College of Science) to integrate "Scientist Spotlights" in several lower-division STEM courses. "Scientist Spotlights" are metacognitive homework assignments that highlight counter-stereotypical scientists. Schinske et al. demonstrated that students who completed these spotlights found personal connections with the highlighted scientists and were then able to describe scientists with counter-stereotypical attributes.[15] These data were exceptionally encouraging because these students were enrolled in an introductory biology course at a diverse community college (De Anza College).

Program structure and culture intervention: sticky situations game

In order to support students in navigating research experiences and the choices they make within those experiences, Dr. Heather Haeger created an activity called *Sticky Situations*. The game has students work through difficult scenarios using a framework for complex decision-making and has teams of students discuss how they would solve problems or respond to microaggressions in research experiences. As students navigate the road through college and beyond, they need to learn the unspoken rules of academia – the hidden curriculum.[16] Though all students benefit from learning the hidden curriculum, taking this curriculum out of hiding is crucial for supporting diversity in higher education. Students of color, low-income, and first-generation college students are less likely to have support systems that know the hidden rules of college.[17] *Sticky Situations* can be used in-class or out-of-class to shed light on the hidden curriculum and support students in developing strategies for navigating complex academic and research situations. This game is designed to complement the Collaborative Institutional Training Initiative (CITI) courses on the Responsible Conduct of Research for undergraduate researchers. Results from pre-/post-tests and student-written reflections on the game illustrate that students feel more confident about navigating academic choices and have fewer misconceptions about undergraduate research after participating in the activity. They also have a lot of fun playing it, and candy is involved. The activity and notes on facilitation are located at the end of the chapter.

Research environment

Our study also found that perception of exclusivity was a barrier for research participation and that there was an inherent bias in the choices faculty made about whom to invite into research. For example, faculty who reach out to students in class about participating in research likely favor students who are more outgoing, who resemble themselves, or are otherwise more relatable to faculty, and who participate more actively in class.[18] Thus, students whose cultures show respect by listening quietly and attentively may be frequently overlooked, and faculty may not realize the implicit biases affecting the students. Students also frequently talked about research only being for the highest-achieving students and for students with concrete academic and career plans. Thus, students who did not think their GPAs were strong enough and/or who had not yet developed clear goals tended to opt out of research. Shifting the norms about who does research and emphasizing that exploration and failure are part of the research process can help shift this expectation.

Research environment intervention: the game of undergraduate research

Games such as *Fair Play* and *REAL LIVES* have been used to foster empathy by allowing players to inhabit the lives of other individuals.[19] At CSUMB, we developed *The Game of Undergraduate Research* in order to share research findings from the present study with faculty regarding the barriers to participation in URSCA or their CUREs. This faculty development activity is an adaptation of *The Game of Life*, a board game where players read through scenarios and roll dice to see which outcome their character will experience. The characters were created from common demographic characteristics (a first-generation college student, or a student whose parents went to college) and situational barriers (having transportation issues, childcare responsibilities, or long commutes). Both the URSCA and CURE versions of the game have participants walk through scenarios in order to explore the potential experiences of undergraduates.

The CURE version of the game has been piloted in the first two iterations of our CURE Faculty Fellows Program, and the URSCA version has been played by approximately 200 faculty and staff at national conferences and at the university.

Seventy-five percent of faculty in the 2019–2020 Fellows cohort said that their participation in the game moderately or significantly influenced their plans to develop their courses. We were also encouraged to see faculty processing how privilege can intersect with undergraduate research opportunities and CURE structures in their reflections. Many faculty were struck by how factors like socioeconomic status, transfer status, or being a parent/caretaker can "stack the deck" and create barriers for students; as one faculty noted, "People with different levels of privilege have different sized margins that allow success or failure. These margins are out of peoples' control."[20] Another faculty member reflected on the ways that intersecting identities and life circumstances can impact student experiences: "It became apparent that some students are very privileged and rarely experience negative results from 'Life.' The game reminded me to take student identity into consideration when setting up the CURE project."[21]

Conclusion

Undergraduate research programs and centers can create more accessible and inclusive research environments for undergraduates through both their direct programing and through trainings and supports they provide to students and faculty on their campus. We encourage you to be creative with the ways you engage in this work, and to feel free to use the games and activities we have developed, which follow this chapter's vignette.

VIGNETTE 12.1   Broadening access through CURE development at the University of Arizona

Kimberly Sierra-Cajas, Senior Director, STEM Equity Systems & Initiatives, and Courtney Leligdon, Undergraduate Research Coordinator, University of Arizona

One program in particular that has made a substantial impact in broadening access to undergraduate research at the University of Arizona (UArizona) is the annual CURE Training Institute (CURETI), designed to provide faculty and instructors information and financial support to develop CUREs.[22] CURETI is a multi-day interactive workshop facilitated by Dr. Sara Brownell, Associate Professor at Arizona State University and leading researcher on the impact of CUREs. Since the first CURETI in 2020, 21 CUREs spanning STEM, humanities, and social sciences have been developed by 29 faculty representing half of the UArizona colleges that offer undergraduate degrees. These CUREs provide authentic research experiences across a wide range of disciplines, from neurology and dendrochronology to civic engagement and political science. During the 2023–2024 academic year, 20 CUREs will be offered with the capacity to reach 1,825 students.

Previously, only faculty and instructors who submitted an application and were awarded funding were invited to attend the CURETI. To promote more widespread understanding of and support for CUREs, the 2023 CURETI was open to faculty and instructors across the university who were interested in learning more about CUREs. Faculty and instructors at Arizona community colleges and tribal colleges were also invited to attend in order to encourage the development of CUREs pre-transfer. Small group breakout sessions were added to facilitate better understanding of the logistics and policies affecting implementation of a CURE, specifically at UArizona. Applications for funding were due several weeks after the Institute so that faculty would have more information on CUREs before submitting their application. Seven teams in attendance were selected to receive funding.

Since spring 2021, 598 undergraduates from 15 different colleges and representing over 140 different majors have completed a CURE at UArizona. Of those students, 27% were first-generation students, 28% were Pell Grant recipients, 46% were from underrepresented ethnic groups, and 65% were female. Additionally, some CUREs offered online increased accessibility of meaningful learning and authentic research experiences for remote students, many of whom were disabled, transportation insecure, or facing other barriers to attending in-person.

Of the students who have taken a CURE, 47% were first- or second-year students. A large contributor to this enrollment is an introductory biology laboratory course required for many STEM students that was gradually converted into a CURE. Previous enrollment data indicates that this course alone has the potential to impact over 1,300 predominantly first- and second-year students each academic year. Since UArizona funded the instructor to attend the Culturally Responsive Curriculum Development Institute, he is implementing culturally responsive practices within the CURE. UArizona is also co-funding the conversion of the same lab course at the local community college to ensure students experience parallel UR experiences before transferring. A recent UArizona assessment of an STEM CURE, $N=258$, showed that taking a CURE significantly increased reported confidence in science skills ($p<0.001$), sense of belonging in science ($p=0.01$), and science identity ($p=0.02$). These factors increase student connection to their STEM major and likelihood of persisting in their degree program, particularly impactful for students early in their undergraduate career.

STICKY SITUATIONS: AN ETHICAL DECISIONMAKING GAME

Heather Haeger, Ph.D.
University of Arizona

Knowing the rules is a start but the next step is making informed decisions in real-life circumstances.

Baird Decision Model: A framework for ethical decision making.
- **Rights and Responsibilities** - Values transparency, future implications focus.
- **Relationships** - Fairness, maintenance of community.
- **Reputation** - Integrity, requirements of your role.
- **Results** - Present and immediate, goal oriented.

Put your ethical decision making to the test

In groups of 5, members take on each of the lenses and Jiminy Cricket.

1. Rights and Responsibilities lens
2. Relationships lens
3. Reputation lens
4. Results lens
5. Jiminy Cricket

Each group member takes 6 pieces of candy (no eating them, yet!)
No candy for Jiminy Cricket

Work through each situation in your group with a representative for each lens and Jiminy Cricket.

Come to a consensus for how to react to each problem. Each representative of a lens has to give-up candy for any concession they make. Jiminy Cricket takes any candy given-up and can call-out members of the group if they are sacrificing their ethics but haven't surrendered their candy.

1 piece of candy = minor repercussions for that lens
2 pieces of candy = major repercussions for that lens

Goal: to keep as much candy as possible!

Problem: The Case of the Changing Voice

GRADUATE RESEARCH ASSISTANT

You are responsible for supervising an undergraduate researcher on a research project. You have noticed portions of a paper you are writing together seem to be written in a much more formal and academic voice than the student usually writes in. You suspect that this student may be plagiarizing. You do not have any proof but have a gut feeling that something is going on.

Issue:
How to ensure the paper you are working on does not include plagiarism and that the researcher you are supervising is behaving ethically.

Problem: The Case of the Microaggressions

UNDERGRADUATE RESEARCHER

You are the only Latina in your research group at a summer REU. You are far from home and your support network. The other students have made comments about your ethnicity asking if you are "illegal" and the PI of your team makes a joke every Tuesday saying "It's Taco Tuesday, where are your tacos?" This seems to be directed to you and not the other students. This makes you feel even more alone and you are considering leaving early and going home without completing the research experience.

Issue:
How to handle this research environment and the decision to stay or leave early?

Problem: The Case of the Last Author

UNDERGRADUATE RESEARCHER

After working on other people's projects for the past year, you are finally allowed to develop and lead your own project. You discuss your ideas with your research mentor and some of the graduate students, but you develop the research questions and protocols. You and another undergraduate researcher collect and analyze the data. When it comes time to present your findings, you see that you are listed as the third author, behind your mentor and a graduate student, and that the other student researcher isn't listed at all.

Issue:
How to manage your relationships with fellow researchers and your mentor while establishing authorship on a project that is already complete.

Problem: The Case of the Fishy Results

UNDERGRADUATE RESEARCHER

You have been working on a research project for 6 months, have presented your findings at conferences in your field, and are in the final revisions of a paper for publication with your research supervisor. The paper has already been accepted for publication pending final edits when you discover inconsistencies in the way that you and the graduate student collected the data. These inconsistencies could affect the findings of the study.

Issue:
How to handle potential errors in the findings you have presented at conferences and are in process of publishing.

Reflection Questions: What was hard, what was easy? Were there lenses that lost their candy first or more often? Were you able to keep all your candy and not give any to Jiminy Cricket? How did you make decisions about what to do or not do?

Figure 12.2 Sticky situations, an ethical decision-making game.

Notes

1 Hurtado, S., et al. "Training Future Scientists: Predicting First-Year Minority Student Participation in Health Science Research." *Research in Higher Education*, vol. 49 no. 2, 2008, 126–152.

Kinzie, J., et al. "Promoting Persistence and Success of Underrepresented Students: Lessons for Teaching and Learning." *New Directions for Teaching and Learning*, vol. 2008 no. 115, 2008, 21–38, https://doi.org/10.1002/tl.323

2 Finley, A., and T. McNair. "Assessing Underserved Students' Engagement in High-Impact Practices." 2013.

3 Haeger, H., et al. "Creating More Inclusive Research Environments for Undergraduates." *Journal of the Scholarship of Teaching and Learning*, vol. 21 no. 1, 2021.

4 Schinske, J.N., et al. "Scientist Spotlight Homework Assignments Shift Students' Stereotypes of Scientists and Enhance Science Identity in a Diverse Introductory Science Class." *CBE—Life Sciences Education*, vol. 15 no. 3, 2016, ar47.

5 Haeger, H., et al. "Navigating the Academic Landscape: How Mentored Research Experiences Can Shed Light on the Hidden Curriculum." *Scholarship and Practice of Undergraduate Research*, vol. 2 no. 1, 2018, 15–23.

6 Kilanowski, J.F. "Breadth of the Socio-Ecological Model." *Journal of Agromedicine*, vol. 22 no. 4, 2017, 295–297.

7 BrckaLorenz, A., et al. "An Examination of Inclusivity and Support for Diversity in STEM Fields." *Journal for STEM Education Research*, vol. 4 no. 3, 2021, 363–379, https://doi.org/10.1007/s41979-021-00055-1

8 Haeger et al.

9 Haeger, H., et al. "Participation in Undergraduate Research at Minority-Serving Institutions." *Perspectives on Undergraduate Research and Mentoring*, vol. 4 no. 1, 2015.

10 Haeger, H., et al. "Participation in Undergraduate Research at Minority-Serving Institutions." *Perspectives on Undergraduate Research and Mentoring*, vol. 4 no. 1, 2015.

11 Nikolova Eddins, S.G., and D.F. Williams. "Based Learning for Undergraduates: A Model for Merger of Research and Undergraduate Education." *Journal on Excellence in College Teaching*, vol. 8 no. 3, 1997, 77–94.
Wilson, A.N., et al. "Making Critical Thinking Visible in Undergraduates' Experiences of Scientific Research." *The Palgrave Handbook of Critical Thinking in Higher Education*. Springer, 2015, pp. 491–508.

12 Hensel, N.H. *Course-Based Undergraduate Research: Educational Equity and High-Impact Practice.* Taylor & Francis, 2023.

13 Lopatto, D. "Survey of Undergraduate Research Experiences (SURE): First Findings." *Cell Biology Education*, vol. 3 no. 4, 2004, 270–277.

14 Kuan, J., and Q.C. Sedlacek. "Does It Matter If I Call It a Cure? Identity Development in Online Entrepreneurship Coursework." *Scholarship and Practice of Undergraduate Research*, vol. 6 no. 1, 2022, 23–31.

15 Schinske, J.N., et al. "Scientist Spotlight Homework Assignments Shift Students' Stereotypes of Scientists and Enhance Science Identity in a Diverse Introductory Science Class." *CBE—Life Sciences Education*, vol. 15 no. 3, 2006, ar47.

16 Conley, D.T. *College Knowledge: What It Really Takes for Students to Succeed and What We Can Do to Get Them Ready.* John Wiley & Sons, 2008.

17 Pascarella, E.T., and P.T. Terenzini. *How College Affects Students: Findings and Insights From Twenty Years of Research.* ERIC, 1991.
Ramirez, E. "'No One Taught Me the Steps': Latinos' Experiences Applying to Graduate School." *Journal of Latinos and Education*, vol. 10 no. 3, 2011, 204–222.

18 Aikens, M.L., et al. "A Social Capital Perspective on the Mentoring of Undergraduate Life Science Researchers: An Empirical Study of Undergraduate–Postgraduate–Faculty Triads." *CBE—Life Sciences Education*, vol. 15 no. 2, 2016, ar16.

19 Gutierrez, B., et al. "'Fair Play': A Videogame Designed to Address Implicit Race Bias Through Active Perspective Taking." *Games for Health Journal*, vol. 3 no. 6, 2014, 371–378.
   Bachen, C.M., et al. "Simulating Real Lives: Promoting Global Empathy and Interest in Learning Through Simulation Games." *Simulation & Gaming*, vol. 43 no. 4, 2012, 437–460.
20 CSUMB CURE Fellows Faculty survey.
21 Instructions for facilitation and the game itself are available in Haeger et al.
22 See https://ur.arizona.edu/cure-training-institute

References

Aikens, M.L., et al. "A Social Capital Perspective on the Mentoring of Undergraduate Life Science Researchers: An Empirical Study of Undergraduate–Postgraduate–Faculty Triads." *CBE—Life Sciences Education*, vol. 15 no. 2, 2016, ar16.

Bachen, C.M., et al. "Simulating Real Lives: Promoting Global Empathy and Interest in Learning Through Simulation Games." *Simulation & Gaming*, vol. 43 no. 4, 2012, 437–460.

BrckaLorenz, A., et al. "An Examination of Inclusivity and Support for Diversity in STEM Fields." *Journal for STEM Education Research*, vol. 4 no. 3, 2021, 363–379, https://doi.org/10.1007/s41979-021-00055-1

Conley, D.T. *College knowledge: What It Really Takes for Students to Succeed and What We Can Do to Get Them Ready.* John Wiley & Sons, 2008.

Finley, A., and T. McNair. *Assessing Underserved Students' Engagement in High-Impact Practices.*

Gutierrez, B., et al. "'Fair Play': A Videogame Designed to Address Implicit Race Bias Through Active Perspective Taking." *Games for Health Journal*, vol. 3 no. 6, 2014, 371–378.

Haeger, H. "Creating More Inclusive Research Environments for Undergraduates." *Journal of the Scholarship of Teaching and Learning*, vol. 21 no. 1, 2021.

Haeger, H., et al. "Participation in Undergraduate Research at Minority-Serving Institutions." *Perspectives on Undergraduate Research and Mentoring*, vol. 4 no. 1, 2015.

Haeger, H., et al. "Navigating the Academic Landscape: How Mentored Research Experiences Can Shed Light on the Hidden Curriculum." *Scholarship and Practice of Undergraduate Research*, vol. 2 no. 1, 2018, 15–23.

Hensel, N.H. *Course-Based Undergraduate Research: Educational Equity and High-Impact Practice.* Taylor & Francis, 2023.

Hurtado, S., et al. "Training Future Scientists: Predicting First-Year Minority Student Participation in Health Science Research." *Research in Higher Education*, vol. 49 no. 2, 2008, 126–152.

Kilanowski, J.F. "Breadth of the Socio-Ecological Model." *Journal of Agromedicine*, vol. 22 no. 4, 2017, 295–297.

Kinzie, J., et al. "Promoting Persistence and Success of Underrepresented Students: Lessons for Teaching and Learning." New *Directions for Teaching and Learning*, vol. 2008 no. 115, 2008, 21–38, https://doi.org/10.1002/tl.323

Kuan, J., and Q.C. Sedlacek. "Does It Matter if I Call It a Cure? Identity Development in Online Entrepreneurship Coursework." *Scholarship and Practice of Undergraduate Research*, vol. 6 no. 1, 2022, 23–31.

Lopatto, D. "Survey of Undergraduate Research Experiences (SURE): First Find-ings." *Cell Biology Education*, vol. 3 no. 4, 2004, 270–277.

Nikolova Eddins, S.G., and D.F. Williams. "Based Learning for Undergraduates: A Model for Merger of Research and Undergraduate Education." *Journal on Excellence in College Teaching*, vol. 8 no. 3, 1997, 77–94.

Pascarella, E.T., and P.T. Terenzini. *How College Affects Students: Findings and Insights from Twenty Years of Research*. ERIC, 1991.

Ramirez, E. "'No One Taught Me the Steps': Latinos' Experiences Applying to Graduate School." *Journal of Latinos and Education*, vol. 10 no. 3, 2011, 204–222.

Schinske, J.N. "Scientist Spotlight Homework Assignments Shift Students' Stereo-types of Scientists and Enhance Science Identity in a Diverse Introductory Science Class." *CBE—Life Sciences Education*, vol. 15 no. 3, 2016, ar47.

Wilson, A.N., et al. "Making Critical Thinking Visible in Undergraduates' Experi-ences of Scientific Research." *The Palgrave Handbook of Critical Thinking in Higher Education*. Springer, 2015, pp. 491–508.

13 Intersecting impact

Aligning meaning-making for undergraduate researchers

The development and support of high-impact practices (HIPS) on most campuses occurs in silos without coordinated connections between these experiences or clear paths for students to either participate in multiple HIPs or build meaningful connections between them. The fact that fewer minoritized students engage in multiple HIPs illustrates the need to create more explicit pathways and intersections between HIPS for students who feel less confident and comfortable navigating the higher education environment.[1] We will explore how undergraduate research, scholarship, and creative activity offices can support students not only in engaging in research but also in making meaning from multiple HIPs. We present three models for engagement across multiple HIPs: **siloed, stacked,** and **intersecting**. We will look closely at the experience of minoritized students at California State University, Monterey Bay (CSUMB), a university that has institutionalized multiple HIPs in the core curriculum, to examine its own progression between these frameworks.

We will present examples of students who have participated in multiple intersecting HIPs, demonstrating how these practices have built-on each other and created a more engaging learning experience that connects students to both meaningful post-graduation career opportunities and to their communities.

Siloed HIPs

In a siloed system, HIPs are designed and experienced without connection between those experiences. Students often only participate in one HIP during their undergraduate career. For the sake of this case study, we are looking at the following HIPs.

- Undergraduate research, scholarship, or creative activities (URSCA).
- Service learning.
- First-year seminar.

DOI: 10.4324/9781003154952-13

- Writing intensive courses.
- ePortfolios.
- Capstone projects.
- Study abroad/global learning.

Though participating in an HIP may be beneficial, this default system of singular experiences does not maximize students' learning and development in college.

Stacked: moving from isolated experiences to multiple HIPs

As institutions seek to increase the learning, development, and retention benefits to students from participating in HIPs, they often structure opportunities for students to participate in multiple HIPs and to track students' participation. Like many institutions, CSUMB has a goal for all students to participate in at least two HIPs before they graduate. They meet this goal by institutionalizing service learning and capstone courses meaning that they are offered as required courses in each degree program and are incorporated into the core curriculum. However, participating in multiple HIPs does not guarantee that students are making connections between them. Additionally, research has demonstrated that institutionalizing stacked HIPs does not necessarily increase student outcomes such as graduation rates.[2] This may be due to adaptations institutions make when they institutionalize HIPs (e.g., decreasing the connection to faculty, rigor of the experience, or individualized experience when HIPs get embedded in the curriculum and required for all students). The limited benefits could also be related to the disconnect between each of the HIP experiences and lack of mechanisms for connecting their experiences in HIPs to each other or to the broader curriculum.

Intersecting HIPs: move from participating in multiple HIPs to creating meaningful intersections among experiences

To move beyond siloed or stacked HIPs, institutions can create meaningful connective tissue that connects these separate experiences and helps students make meaning out of these experiences. This involves opportunities for students to connect their experiences in and out of the classroom and to identify transferable skills that apply across experiences. Creating intersections can be done informally through discussions with students about their experiences in different HIPs or systematically through ePortfolios or transcript systems that ask students to track and reflect on their experiences.

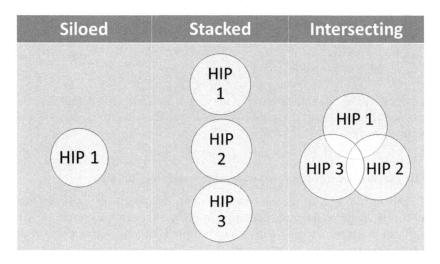

Siloed	Stacked	Intersecting

Figure 13.1 Siloed, stacked, and intersecting HIPs.

The following section will provide student examples about how students make these connections (or not) and how a centralized URSCA office can support building these connections. We also provide a vignette about how universities use the Student Transformative Learning Record to facilitate intersecting HIP experiences.

Creating connections: the student experience

To illustrate how different alignments, or lack thereof, are experienced, we will present a series of student experiences and how they made sense of their HIP experiences. We have changed student names and modified details to protect their anonymity. The Institutional Review Board (IRB) at California State University, Monterey Bay (CSUMB) reviews the protocol for interviews with students and determined it does not qualify as human subjects research because the primary goal of the interviews was for programmatic improvement. All the students from this case study attended CSUMB between 2016 and 2018.

Juan: Biology Major. Participated in two semesters of **Service Learning**, two years of **Research**, multiple **Writing Intensive** courses as an English language learner, and a **Senior Capstone**.

Service and research to support migrant farming communities

Juan participated in Service Learning in the Center for the Health Assessment of Mothers and Children of Salinas (CHAMACOS), a UC-Berkeley study. The CHAMACOS study is a longitudinal birth cohort study examining chemicals and other factors in the environment and children's health from the Salinas Valley. During community events, he shared information with fieldworkers about how to protect their families from pesticides exposure at work.

At the time, Juan was also participating in research at the United States Department of Agriculture (USDA) in Salinas, CA. The goal of the investigation was to use specific bacteria's toxins (bacteriocins) produced during competition for nutrients to replace pesticides. This pesticide alternative would control plant diseases and pests in a way that is nontoxic to animals, humans, and the environment.

Research on alternatives to pesticides was presented as his senior capstone.

Making the connection

> "I figured out that my research and volunteer service site were connected due to my community experience and academic knowledge. As a son of field workers, I have observed the connections between some agricultural unsustainable practices and the environmental issues it generates for some underprivileged group of people which may lead to future health problems and a poor quality of life."

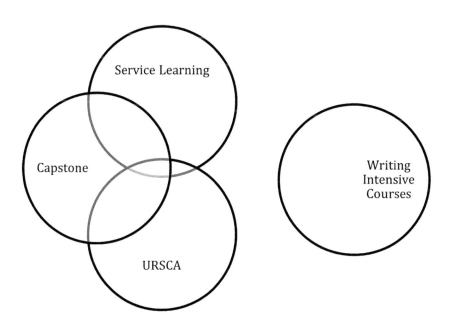

Figure 13.2 Intersecting HIPs: service and research to support migrant farming communities.

Juan was able to build connections between service learning, research, and capstone, but did not see the relationship to his writing intensive courses despite extensive writing about his research.

Impact on the future

After graduation, Juan was offered a position as a lab technician testing agricultural soil samples for pathogens and has since completed a Master of Science degree. Juan was also awarded the Sally Casanova Pre-Doctoral Fellowship which funded him to conduct research with faculty at UC Davis the summer before he started graduate school.

Alyssa: Biology Major. Participated in a **First-year Seminar** course, two semesters of **Service Learning**, two years of **Research**, multiple **Writing Intensive Courses**, and **Senior Capstone**.

Service and research to support health

"My research focus was the molecular mechanisms of lifestyle diseases (such as obesity, diabetes, and cardiovascular disease) while my service learning was educating students about nutrition to prevent such conditions. I spent my first summer of research at the University of Toledo in a diabetes research center where I studied type two diabetes mellitus and atherosclerosis. To conclude my summer, I attended an international conference where my mentor spoke about her research but more importantly showed a picture of an obese child consuming a large hamburger. Drawing the crowd's attention to nutrition as a key mediator of these diseases. I quickly realized a gap existed between scientific research and the translation of the science into community education. The following semesters I was looking for a service-learning site and found Kids Eat Right doing just that. My service learning was teaching 4th grade students about nutrition and exercise. Cells, animal models, and protein mechanisms fascinate me; however, the broader impact of my research as an undergraduate was educating the public-school students about preventing disease in the first place."

Alyssa also used her research for her senior capstone.

Making the connection

"I made the connection between my service and my research myself but the service class I took facilitated it. . . . When choosing a service

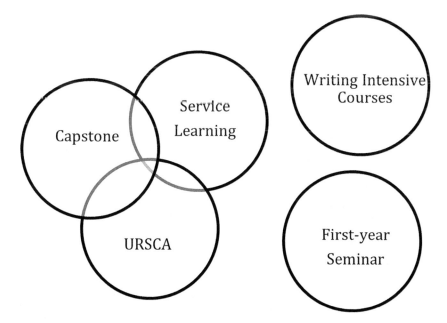

Figure 13.3 Intersecting HIPs service and research to support health.

site [the professor] had us think about what kind of career we were interested in after graduation. For example, if we were interested in becoming a dentist she suggested seeking out a dentist office. So, when I chose my site originally, it was to gain experience regarding a career field and mine just happened to be a research professor. So naturally when [the professor] mentioned to me a woman from the Community Hospital of the Monterey Peninsula was looking for students to help with nutrition education, I knew it matched my research and career interests."

Like Juan, Alyssa also found that connections between service learning and URSCA happened organically since both were connected to her career interests, and she was also able to utilize her research in the capstone course. She did not see connections between the first-year seminar course or writing intensive courses she took.

Impact on the future

Alyssa was awarded the Sally Casanova Pre-Doctoral Fellowship which funded her to conduct research with faculty at the University of Washington the summer after her graduation. She is now working as a research assistant and pursuing her Ph.D. in Molecular Medicine and Mechanisms of Disease at the University of Washington.

Carla: Psychology major, service-learning minor. Participated in a service-focused **First-year Seminar**, two semesters of **Service Learning**, a service-focused **Writing Intensive** course, and **Capstone**. Her service-focused first-year seminar, writing course, and course-based peer leadership program inspired a capstone about impact on sense of belonging for minoritized students.

Service-driven HIPs

Citing work by Sylvia Hurtado and Deborah Faye Carter (1997) in her capstone research, Carla personally related to findings about the importance of students of color feeling a sense of belonging on college campuses:

> "I was ready to transfer after my first semester, but my FYS service activities, and my writing and service learning classes about educational equity not only helped me see that my experiences before college were real, but I also learned a vocabulary, theory and concepts that made me want to educate others. Doing service in the community allowed me to actually incorporate things I was learning."

Carla's insights were echoed by other students in her capstone project, a qualitative analysis about the impact of service learning on students of color. In her summary, she notes three emerging themes based on interviews: 1) that service learning helped students of color better understand oppression, 2) that service learning supported their own identity development, and 3) that service learning helped establish a sense of belonging both on campus and in the surrounding community. She notes "It [service learning] makes me feel like a part of the solution rather than a problem. I can see myself in some of the kids and I feel as if now I have the opportunity to help them."

Making the connection

> "I hadn't thought about this, but having several courses that connected me to service not only shaped my career interests, but they also helped inspire me to start a Delta Sigma Theta chapter on campus. Growing up, a lot of my mentors were Deltas, who are all about service. I did service but never really thought about what it was or what it really meant. After learning more through my courses, I wanted to be a Delta even more, and it made me want to charter it here at CSUMB. It's created another space for African American women on campus."

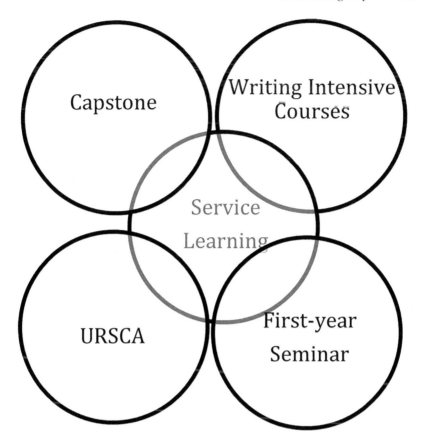

Figure 13.4 Intersecting HIPs service and research to support a sense of belonging.

The fact that Carla's experiences in URSCA, writing, first-year seminar, and capstone all centered around service and connected to service learning structured intersections through all her HIP experiences.

Impact on the future

Carla graduated and served as an AmeriCorps VIP at CSU-Monterey Bay, as the Program Coordinator of the Service Learning Student Leadership program. Carla plans to attend graduate school in the field of social work after completing her AmeriCorps assignment.

Stacked and intersecting HIPs

The students in these examples demonstrate that students are creating connections between some of their HIP experiences and do not see the interconnections of others. The examples also illustrate the impact of partnerships in the local community that speak to students' interests. The most common connections were with service learning. As an office, having discussions with the staff or faculty leading service learning on campus about how to identify service-learning opportunities that connect to some of the URSCA opportunities you support can further create that intersection. Building opportunities to make connections into HIPs at your institution can create a model for students to see the intersection and build transferable skills across experiences.

Questions for your institution:

- What is the meaningful "connective tissue" that connects these separate HIP experiences? For majority students and for minoritized students? How is the "connective tissue" distinct for minoritized students?
- What processes help students connect the dots across separate HIP experiences?
- What programs or initiatives are intentional about connecting HIP experiences?
- How can institutions help minoritized students recognize their own AGENCY to connect HIPs more intentionally?

Creating connections through research abroad

John E. Banks, California State University, Monterey Bay

General overview and background: CSU-LSAMP Research Expedition

Launched in 2011 and led by faculty and staff from California State University, Monterey Bay, the CSU-LSAMP Costa Rica Research Expedition program immerses students in the study of tropical environments and biological diversity, statistics and research methods, current issues in conservation, and Costa Rican geography and culture. Students receive instruction in the development of research questions, fundamentals of experimental design, sampling, hypothesis testing, and the responsible conduct of research, while engaging in hands-on activities across a wide variety of habitats and landscapes. The course has evolved several times over the several years, ranging from two- to ten-week courses of study for students with little or no research experience to engage with group and individual research activities in terrestrial and marine/aquatic environments. The course combines global learning with research immersion, providing students with a unique opportunity to engage in "stacked" HIPs, which has been shown to synergistically boost student scholarly identity, persistence, and engagement.[3]

The course is open to CSU-LSAMP students from across the CSU system; since its inception, the CSU-LSAMP Costa Rica course has welcomed over 100 student participants from CSU Channel Islands, Chico, Dominguez Hills, East Bay, Fresno, Fullerton, Humboldt, Los Angeles, Monterey Bay, Pomona, Sacramento, San Bernardino, San Diego, San Jose, San Luis Obispo, Sonoma, and Stanislaus. Many of the student participants over the years have gone on to present their independent research at national conferences. Furthermore, many students often go on to conduct other research projects – not necessarily related to the work they did in the course.

Over the years, course activities have taken place in a wide variety of habitats, including the cloud forest of Monteverde, the coffee highlands of Tarrazú, the rural village of Mastatal adjacent to La Cangreja National Park, and the coastal environments of Quepos/Manuel Antonio and the Cabo Blanco Absolute Reserve on the Nicoya peninsula. Students have worked on individual as well as on group research projects in several habitats. Student independent research projects over the years have ranged widely according to their interests and curiosity.

In 2022 and 2023, CSU-LSAMP students participated in two and a half week expeditions focused on a group research project in the village of Mastatal (pop. 150), learning about ecology, experimental design, statistical methods, and field techniques for sampling, sorting, and cataloging arthropods. The expedition was bookended by a few days learning about sustainable coffee production and the coastal environment.

The first part of the expedition took place in Santa Maria de Dota, a small town in the coffee highlands in the world-famous Tarrazú region. Activities included a tour of the nearby CoopeDota production facilities (including coffee tasting, or "cupping") along with lectures and discussions that served as an introduction to ecological concepts pertaining to sustainable coffee as well as a refresher/introduction to some statistics. The visit also featured a visit to a working coffee farm to collect some data on bean production; the group then analyzed using some of the statistical methods we learned in order to test hypotheses about coffee pollination and habitat diversity.

The main phase of the expedition took place in the small rural village of Mastatal carrying out a research project in the shadow of La Cangreja National Park. Our project, a follow-up of a project conducted with students in the same sites nearly 20 years ago, aims to compare the relative contribution of farmland and forests to arthropod biodiversity. This entailed spending six days of each expedition setting pitfall traps, characterizing ground and canopy cover, and collecting, sorting, photographing, and measuring the body sizes of beetle and spider specimens from several sites around the region. Specimens were sent to colleagues who are taxonomic specialists in San Jose for further identification; we used specialized software to analyze the specimen photographs, measuring body and leg sizes of the beetles and spiders in order to better understand traits like mobility and predator size as potential drivers of abundance and diversity patterns. Data from the expeditions are being combined to create a follow-up article to be submitted to a peer-reviewed journal. River crossings, steep hillsides, and the usual assortment of biting insects along with the occasional torrential downpour were among the challenges the group faced; all came through with flying colors and emerged with some hard-won tropical field ecology experience. In between the hard work in the field and lab, students enjoyed playing pick-up soccer, touring the local family-run cacao farm and chocolate producer, learning about medicinal plants from an indigenous medicine man, eating dinner at the village "soda" (small restaurant), and hiking to local waterfalls. The expedition wrapped up with a visit to the coast, where the group enjoyed a guided wildlife tour of Manuel Antonio National Park and explored nearby mangroves via kayak.

Notes

1 Haeger, H., et al. "Participation in Undergraduate Research at Minority Serving Institutions." *Perspectives on Undergraduate Research and Mentoring*, vol. 4 no. 1, 2015, http://blogs.elon.edu/purm/files/2015/11/Haeger-et-al-PURM-4.1-1.pdf
2 Johnson, S.R., and F.K. Stage. "Academic Engagement and Student Success: Do High-Impact Practices Mean Higher Graduation Rates?" *The Journal of Higher Education*, vol. 89 no. 5, 2018, 753–781, https://doi.org/10.1080/00221546.2018.1441107
3 Banks, J.E., and J.J. Gutiérrez. "Undergraduate Research in International Settings: Synergies in Stacked High-Impact Practices." *CUR Quarterly*, vol. 37 no. 3, 2017, 18–26.
   Dong, W., et al. "Effects of Research-Related Activities on Graduation at a Hispanic Serving Institution." *Journal of College Student Retention: Research, Theory & Practice*, vol. 26 no. 1, 2021, https://doi.org/10.1177/15210251211065099

References

Banks, J.E., and J.J. Gutiérrez. "Undergraduate Research in International Settings: Synergies in Stacked High-Impact Practices." *CUR Quarterly*, vol. 37 no. 3, 2017, 18–26.

Dong, W., et al. "Effects of Research-Related Activities on Graduation at a Hispanic Serving Institution." *Journal of College Student Retention: Research, Theory & Practice*, vol. 26 no. 1, 2021, https://doi.org/10.1177/15210251211065099 1

Haeger, H. "Participation in Undergraduate Research at Minority Serving Institutions." *Perspectives on Undergraduate Research and Mentoring*, vol. 4 no. 1, 2015.

Hurtado, S., and D.F. Carter. "Effects of College Transition and Perceptions of the Campus Racial Climate on Latino College Students' Sense of Belonging." *Sociology of Education*, vol. 70, 1997, 324–345.

Johnson, S.R., and F.K. Stage. "Academic Engagement and Student Success: Do High-Impact Practices Mean Higher Graduation Rates?" *The Journal of Higher Education*, vol. 89 no. 5, 2018, 753–781, https://doi.org/10.1080/00221546.2 018.1441107

14 Resources to engage in the community of URSCA scholars and practitioners

We hope this book has been useful in getting you started on your journey to establish an undergraduate research, scholarship, and creative activities (URSCA) office/center/program. As you build support for URSCA on your campus, remember that you embark on these efforts as part of a community of scholars and practitioners. In addition to the practical advice we offer in this book, there are a number of other volumes and resources we recommend adding to your library – some of which expand on questions addressed in our book, others of which address issues in undergraduate research for different audiences. We list a small sample of these below – these are the books, journals, and resources we recommend you start with – with many more available in the bibliography.

Joining a community of research on URSCA

You can participate in the community of scholars and practitioners actively engaged in URSCA through current research on best practices in research. Here are two journals that specifically focus on research about URSCA.

Scholarship and Practice of Undergraduate Research (SPUR), www.cur. org/what/publications/journals/spur/issues/
Perspectives on Undergraduate Research and Mentoring (PURM), www. elon.edu/u/academics/undergraduate-research/purm/

Both SPUR and PURM include empirical research on effective practices in URSCA, examples of specific programs, and literature reviews on specific topics within URSCA. The journals offer relevant research related to creating and sustaining engaging and equitable research experiences for students, along with research about how to support mentors and incentivize faculty engagement in URSCA.

In addition to these journals that focus exclusively on URSCA, many disciplinary education journals regularly publish research related to URSCA in their

DOI: 10.4324/9781003154952-14

field. For example, the CBE-Life Sciences Education journal (www.lifescied. org/) has published hundreds of articles on URSCA in the sciences. Searching for journals in your discipline or the disciplines that your students are in can provide models for effective practice and creative ways to engage students and faculty in URSCA at your institution. Journals that focus on higher education and the Scholarship of Teaching and Learning (https://scholarworks. iu.edu/journals/index.php/josotl/about) also frequently feature research about URSCA across disciplines. Additionally, as you grow your URSCA office and conduct assessment of your programs, you might consider what ways you can contribute to this community of scholars and publish case studies about programs you create, or research based on your assessment results.

Students in your URSCA program can also publish their research in a number of journals that publish student work. The Council on Undergraduate Research (CUR) keeps an active list of journals that are accepting student publications (www.cur.org/resources-publications/student-resources/ student-journals/undergraduate-research-journal-listing/).

Engaging with books and other publications

Numerous books, white papers, and edited volumes are available to support your URSCA office development. We recommend the following books for considering how undergraduate research functions as part of a connected system of HIPs and how to structure these opportunities to increase educational equity.

Hensel, Nancy, with Cathy Davidson. *Course-Based Undergraduate Research: Educational Equity and High-Impact Practice.* Stylus, 2018. Co-published with the Council for Undergraduate Research.

Kinzie, J., et al. *Delivering on the Promise of High-Impact Practices: Research and Models for Achieving Equity, Fidelity, Impact, and Scale.* Stylus Publishing, LLC, 2022.

CUR also has a number of publications to explore. They have a system for evaluating your campus's level of support for URSCA and a publication on best practices through the Characteristics of Excellence in Undergraduate Research (COEUR) website (www.cur.org/resources-publications/characteristics-of-excellence-in-undergraduate-research-coeur/) and publication.

Characteristics of Excellence in Undergraduate Research (CUR, ed. Nancy Hensel, 2012) www.cur.org/assets/1/23/COEUR_final.pdf

Additionally, CUR also has over 20 handbooks and whitepapers available for free or reduced price to CUR members (https://myaccount. cur.org/bookstore). Some specific publications we found helpful are listed later.

Kinkead, Joyce, and Linda Blockus. *Undergraduate Research Offices and Programs: Models and Practices.* Council on Undergraduate Research, 2012.

Klos, Naomi Yavneh, et al., editors. *Creative Inquiry in the Arts and Humanities: Models of Undergraduate Research.* The Council on Undergraduate Research, 2011.

The present book is part of a Routledge series on undergraduate research which offers a number of books focused on URSCA in specific disciplines and offers guides for students and for faculty (www.routledge.com/Routledge-Undergraduate-Research-Series/book-series/RURS). We also found *Undergraduate Research for Student Engagement and Learning* by Josh Murray (2018) informative and use *Critical Mentoring: A Practical Guide* by Torie Weiston-Serdan (2023) for faculty reading groups or mentoring communities of practice. The *Cambridge Handbook of Undergraduate Research* (Mieg et al., 2022) is another useful resource for informing the activities of your URSCA office or for individual faculty interested in mentoring students. This handbook draws on international perspectives to inform URSCA development in different educational contexts. Nancy Hensel's 2021 book, *Undergraduate Research at Community Colleges: Equity, Discovery, and Innovation,* also specifically addresses how URSCA can be supported at community colleges.

Hensel, N.H. *Undergraduate Research at Community Colleges: Equity, Discovery, and Innovation.* Routledge, 2021. ISBN 9781620369951

Mieg, H., et al., editors. *The Cambridge Handbook of Undergraduate Research (Cambridge Handbooks in Education).* Cambridge University Press, 2022, https://doi.org/10.1017/9781108869508

Murray. *Undergraduate Research for Student Engagement and Learning.* Routledge, 2018, https://doi-org.ezproxy4.library.arizona.edu/10.4324/9781315692159

Weiston-Serdan, T. *Critical Mentoring: A Practical Guide.* Stylus, 2017.

Connecting in-person and virtually

In addition to engaging with the literature and research on URSCA, we also encourage you to get involved in virtual and in-person conversations about best practices. There are many ways to do this, but we find ourselves most energized when we attend and present at conferences and engage in communities of practice, both in person and online. We recommend conferences like the annual Council on Undergraduate Research (CUR) conference (ConnectUR), and those of the American Association of Colleges and Universities (AAC&U), the Alliance for Hispanic Serving Institution

Educators (AHSIE), and the American Educational Research Association (AERA). For those interested in URSCA within the context of other high-impact practices (HIPs), we also recommend the HIPs in the States track at the Assessment Institute in Indianapolis (IUPUI). For those interested in CURES and URSCA at the two year college level, we recommend connecting with the Community College Undergraduate Research Initiative (CCURI) and CUREnet.

However, you choose to join the conversation, remember that you are not alone in your work. Within your campus, and the broader URSCA community there are allies, sources of support, and inspiration for new ideas. We hope that reading this book serves as a launching point for your URSCA center/program and are excited to be in community with you.

Index

Note: Page numbers in italics indicate a figure on the corresponding page.

Howard Hughes Medical Institute
60, 66
HSI *see* Hispanic-Serving Institution
Huerta, Andrew 11–13
Hurtado, Sylvia 158

Idea Network of Biomedical Research
Excellence (INBRE) 41
IDI-Lab 143
implicit bias 85, 145
imposter phenomenon 43, 72, 75–76,
85, 128n1
inclusivity, conceptual model of *141*
inequality, disrupting patterns of 2–4
institutional bureaucracy: navigating
108–119; databases and
information tracking 114–115;
funding research supplies 113;
funding student travel 113–114;
paying students 111–113; student
research placements 108–111;
understanding 108; vignettes
115–119
International Research Experience for
Students (IRES) 42
intersecting impact 152–162; *see also*
HIPs
intersectionalities 13
Introduction to Research & Creative
Scholarship Opportunities
(INTROs) 30
Isola, Zia 92

Juvera, Victoria 11–13

Kids Eat Right 156
Koret Foundation 60, 64

Leadership Alliance 78, 93, 99n7
Leligdon, Courtney 146–147
Lopez, Holly 11–13
Los Angeles Valley College (LAVC)
68–69
Louis Stokes Alliance for Minority
Participation (LSAMP) program
37; CSU-LSAMP alliance 21;
CSU-LSAMP Research Expedition
160–162; National Science
Foundation Louis Stokes Alliance
for Minority Participation (NSF
LSAMP) Program 73

MacMeans, Tianna 11–13
Manuel Antonio National Park
161–162
Maryville College 104
McMahon, Trina 75
McNair Post-Baccalaureate
Achievement Program 19–21,
28, 30, 37, 41, 43, 56, 57, 64,
73, 142
Mellon Foundation 59–60, 66
mentee support 90–91; *see also*
mentor-mentee relationships
Mentorcollective platform 34, 46n1
Mentoring 101 skill module 92
mentor-mentee agreement (sample) 75,
93, 95–98
mentor-mentee relationships 35,
74–75; acknowledgement and
motivation in 89; determining the
structure of 85–87; establishing
expectations in 89; facilitating
83–98; maintaining 92
mentors: co-mentors 93–94;
communicating with 72;
compensation and recognition
of 102; distributed 118; external
110–111; faculty 1, 5–6, 36, 40,
44, 51, 77, 79, 83–85, 106; Faculty
Mentor Stars 44; faculty and
research 34–35; finding funding
to support 55–70; on-site 118;
potential 74–75, 83, 86–87, 109;
research 48–49; selection of 91;
showcasing 49; student research
32–33; supporting 101; support
strategies 100–106; undergraduate
research 41
mentorship and mentoring 5, 9, 19,
22; at Caltech 93–94; effective 85;
disciplinary inclusion and 9–11;
ending relationship 90; importance
of 83; inclusive 84–85, 92; models
of 83; peer 36; philosophy of 88;
research and mentoring programs
32; Research and Mentoring
Program, Valencia 28; skill module
in 92; structured programs in 34;
vignette 93–94
mentor training 88–90; understanding
mentees 88
MindTools 75